MARVEL
ULTIMATE
SPIDER-MAN

MARVEL UNIVERSE ULTIMATE SPIDER-MAN VOL. 7. Contains material originally published in magazine form as MARVEL UNIVERSE ULTIMATE SPIDER-MAN #25-28. First printing 2014. ISBN# 978-0-7851-8974-9. Published by MARVEL WORLDWIDE, INC., a subsidiary of MARVEL ENTERTAINMENT, LLC. OFFICE OF PUBLICATION: 135 West 50th Street, New York, NY 10020. Copyright © 2014 Marvel Characters, Inc. All rights reserved. All characters featured in this issue and the distinctive names and likenesses thereof, and all related indicia are trademarks of Marvel Characters, Inc. No similarity between any of the names, characters, persons, and/or institutions in this magazine with those of any living or dead person or institution is intended, and any such similarity which may exist is purely coincidental. Printed in the U.S.A. ALAN FINE, EVP - Office of the President, Marvel Worldwide, Inc. and EVP & CMO Marvel Characters B.V.; DAN BUCKLEY, Publisher & President - Print, Animation & Digital Divisions; JOE QUESADA, Chief Creative Officer; TOM BREVOORT, SVP of Publishing; DAVID BOGART, SVP of Operations & Procurement, Publishing; C.B. CEBULSKI, SVP of Creator & Content Development; DAVID GABRIEL, SVP Print, Sales & Marketing; JIM O'KEEFE, VP of Operations & Logistics; DAN CARR, Executive Director of Publishing Technology; SUSAN CRESPI, Editorial Operations Manager; ALEX MORALES, Publishing Operations Manager; STAN LEE, Chairman Emeritus. For information regarding advertising in Marvel Comics or on Marvel.com, please contact Niza Disla, Director of Marvel Partnerships, at ndisla@marvel.com. For Marvel subscription inquiries, please call 800-217-9158. Manufactured between 8/1/2014 and 9/8/2014 by SHERIDAN BOOKS, INC., CHELSEA, MI, USA.

10 9 8 7 6 5 4 3 2 1

MARVEL
ULTIMATE
SPIDER-MAN

BASED ON THE TV SERIES BY
**MAN OF ACTION,
BRIAN MICHAEL BENDIS,
SCOTT MOSIER, DANIELLE WOLFF &
RICH FOGEL**

ADAPTED BY
JOE CARAMAGNA

EDITOR
SEBASTIAN GIRNER

CONSULTING EDITOR
JON MOISAN

SENIOR EDITOR
MARK PANICCIA

SPECIAL THANKS TO SANDY SIRIRAT,
MARVEL ANIMATION & PRODUCT FACTORY

Collection Editor: **Sarah Brunstad**
Associate Managing Editor: **Alex Starbuck**
Editors, Special Projects: **Jennifer Grünwald & Mark D. Beazley**
Senior Editor, Special Projects: **Jeff Youngquist**
SVP Print, Sales & Marketing: **David Gabriel**
Head of Marvel Television: **Jeph Loeb**

Editor In Chief: **Axel Alonso**
Chief Creative Officer: **Joe Quesada**
Publisher: **Dan Buckley**
Executive Producer: **Alan Fine**

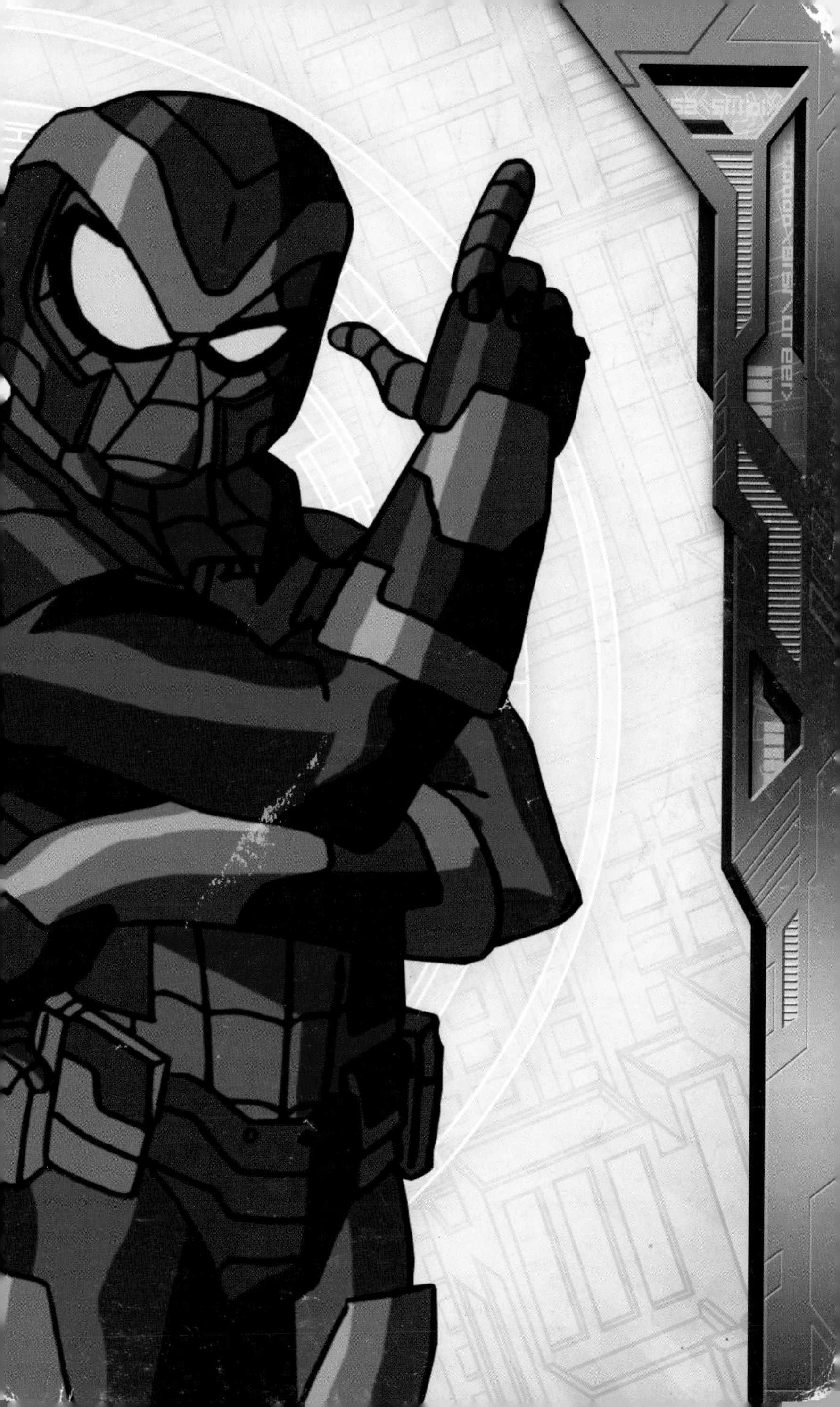

While attending a radiology demonstration, high school student Peter Parker was bitten by a radioactive spider and gained the spider's powers! Now he is training with a superspy organization called S.H.I.E.L.D. to become the...

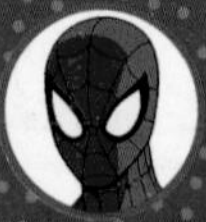

Spider-Man

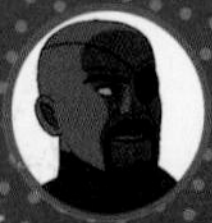

Nick Fury

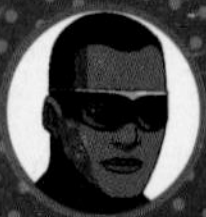

Luke Cage

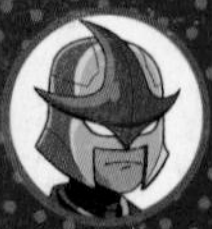

Nova

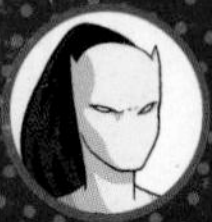

White Tiger

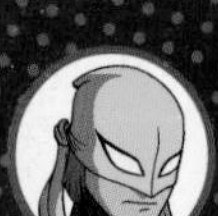

Iron Fist

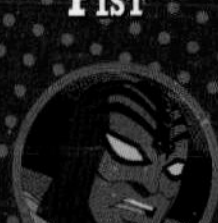

Scorpio

MARVEL

ULTIMATE SPIDER-MAN™

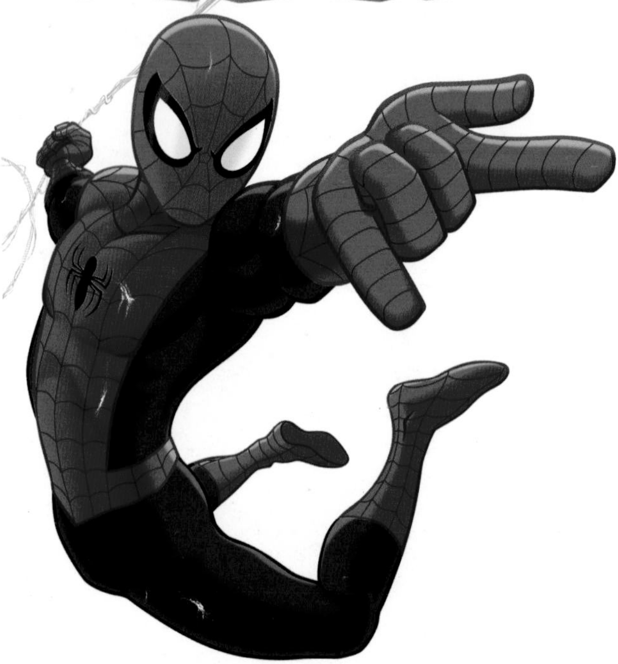

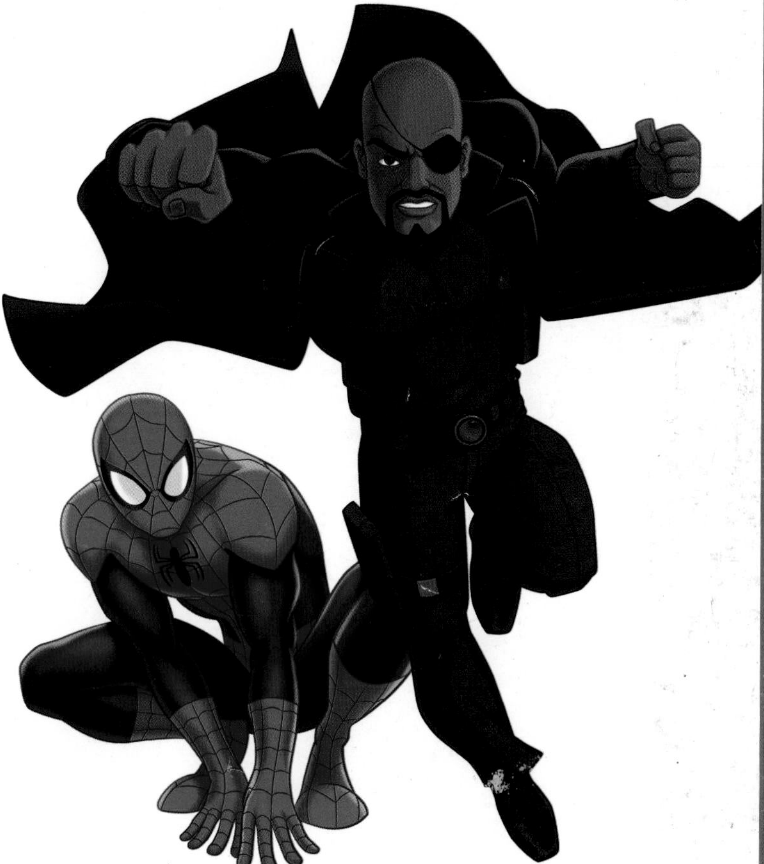

25

Based on "For Your Eye Only"

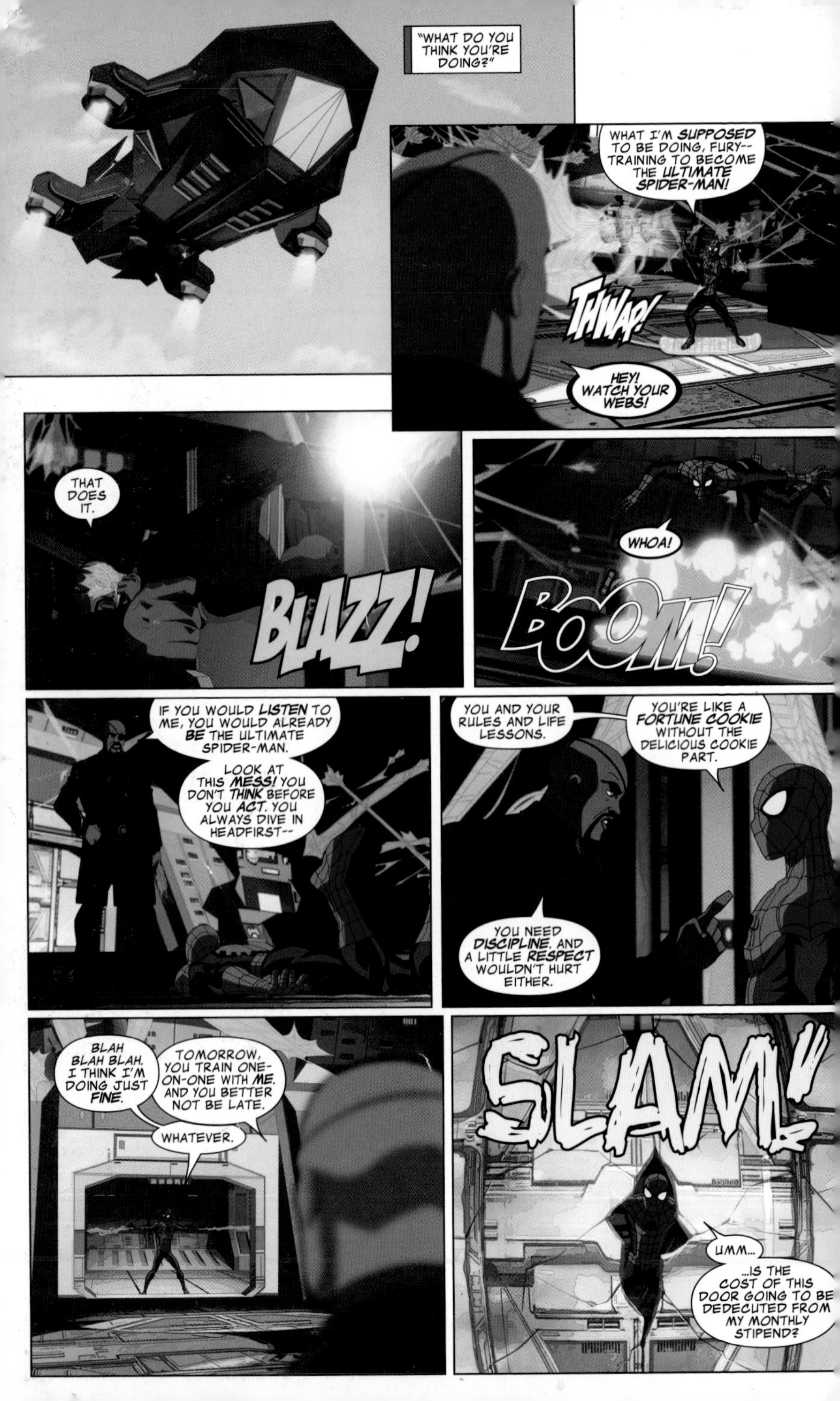
"WHAT DO YOU THINK YOU'RE DOING?"
WHAT I'M SUPPOSED TO BE DOING, FURY-- TRAINING TO BECOME THE ULTIMATE SPIDER-MAN!
THWAP!
HEY! WATCH YOUR WEBS!
THAT DOES IT.
BLAZZ!
WHOA!
BOOM!
IF YOU WOULD LISTEN TO ME, YOU WOULD ALREADY BE THE ULTIMATE SPIDER-MAN.
LOOK AT THIS MESS! YOU DON'T THINK BEFORE YOU ACT. YOU ALWAYS DIVE IN HEADFIRST--
YOU AND YOUR RULES AND LIFE LESSONS.
YOU'RE LIKE A FORTUNE COOKIE WITHOUT THE DELICIOUS COOKIE PART.
YOU NEED DISCIPLINE. AND A LITTLE RESPECT WOULDN'T HURT EITHER.
BLAH BLAH BLAH. I THINK I'M DOING JUST FINE.
TOMORROW, YOU TRAIN ONE-ON-ONE WITH ME. AND YOU BETTER NOT BE LATE.
WHATEVER.
SLAM!
UMM...
...IS THE COST OF THIS DOOR GOING TO BE DEDECUTED FROM MY MONTHLY STIPEND?

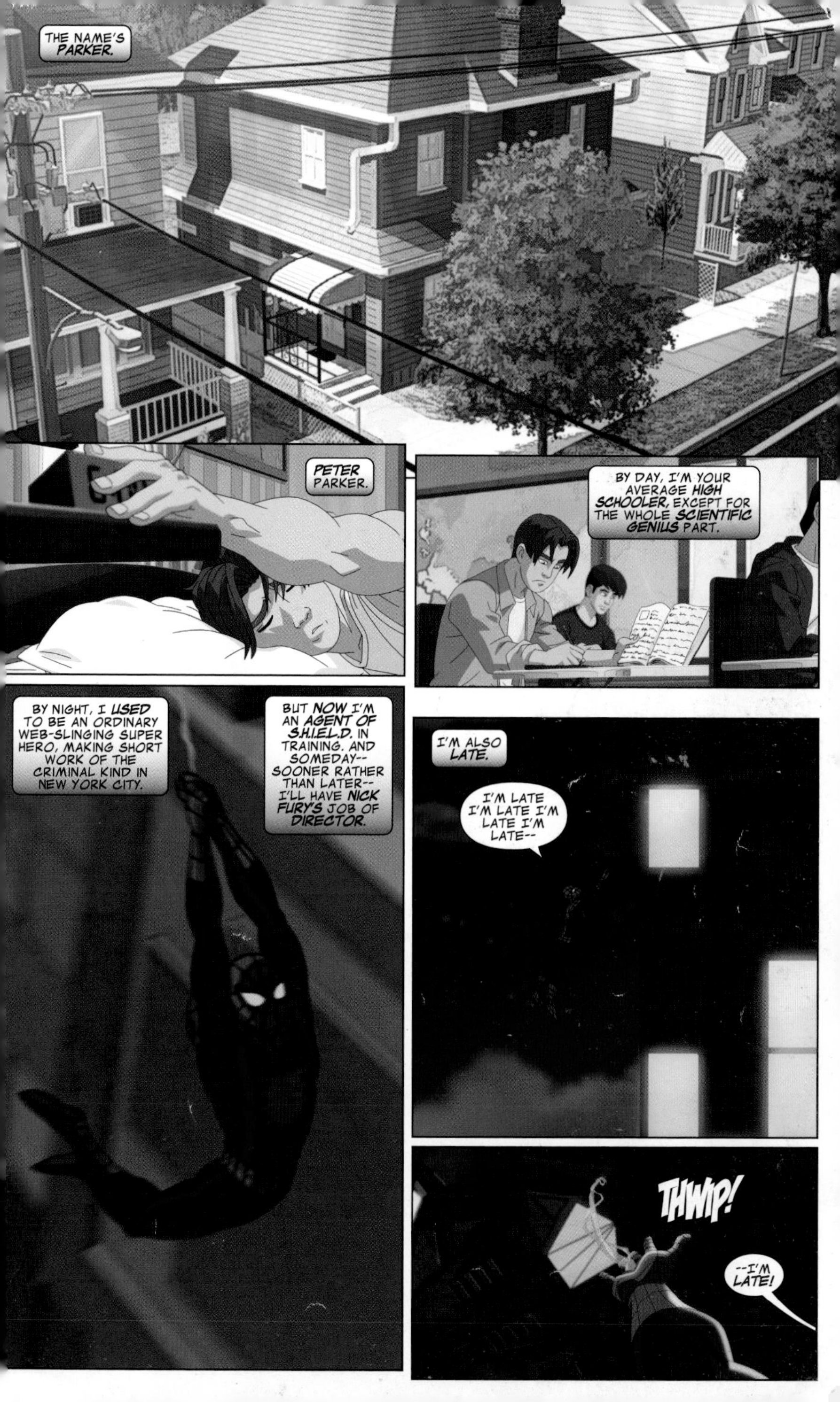
THE NAME'S PARKER.
PETER PARKER.
BY DAY, I'M YOUR AVERAGE HIGH SCHOOLER, EXCEPT FOR THE WHOLE SCIENTIFIC GENIUS PART.
BY NIGHT, I USED TO BE AN ORDINARY WEB-SLINGING SUPER HERO, MAKING SHORT WORK OF THE CRIMINAL KIND IN NEW YORK CITY.
BUT NOW I'M AN AGENT OF S.H.I.E.L.D. IN TRAINING. AND SOMEDAY-- SOONER RATHER THAN LATER-- I'LL HAVE NICK FURY'S JOB OF DIRECTOR.
I'M ALSO LATE.
I'M LATE I'M LATE I'M LATE I'M LATE--
THWIP!
--I'M LATE!

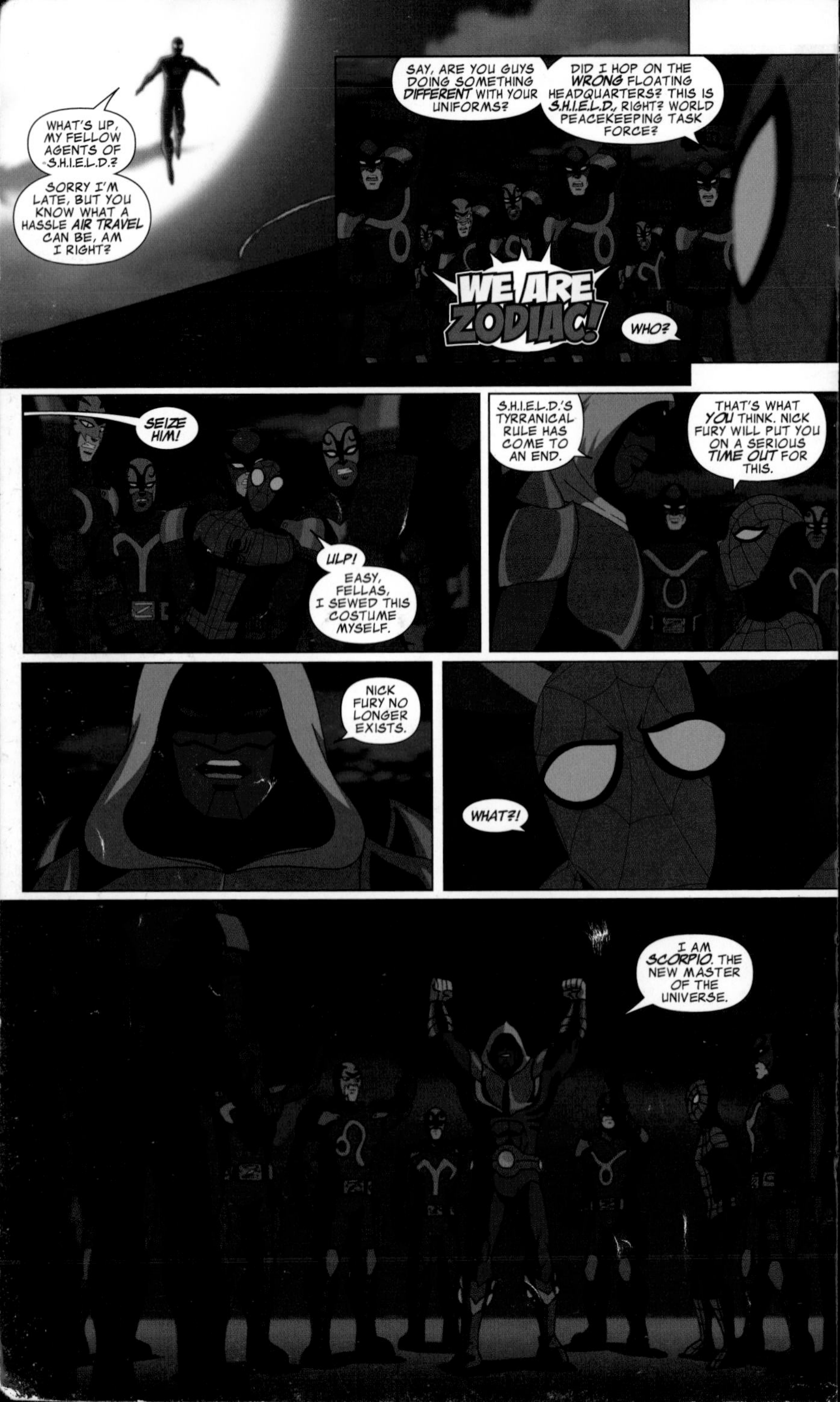
WHAT'S UP, MY FELLOW AGENTS OF S.H.I.E.L.D.?
SORRY I'M LATE, BUT YOU KNOW WHAT A HASSLE AIR TRAVEL CAN BE, AM I RIGHT?
SAY, ARE YOU GUYS DOING SOMETHING DIFFERENT WITH YOUR UNIFORMS?
DID I HOP ON THE WRONG FLOATING HEADQUARTERS? THIS IS S.H.I.E.L.D., RIGHT? WORLD PEACEKEEPING TASK FORCE?
WE ARE ZODIAC!
WHO?
SEIZE HIM!
ULP! EASY, FELLAS, I SEWED THIS COSTUME MYSELF.
S.H.I.E.L.D.'S TYRRANICAL RULE HAS COME TO AN END.
THAT'S WHAT YOU THINK. NICK FURY WILL PUT YOU ON A SERIOUS TIME OUT FOR THIS.
NICK FURY NO LONGER EXISTS.
WHAT?!
I AM SCORPIO. THE NEW MASTER OF THE UNIVERSE.

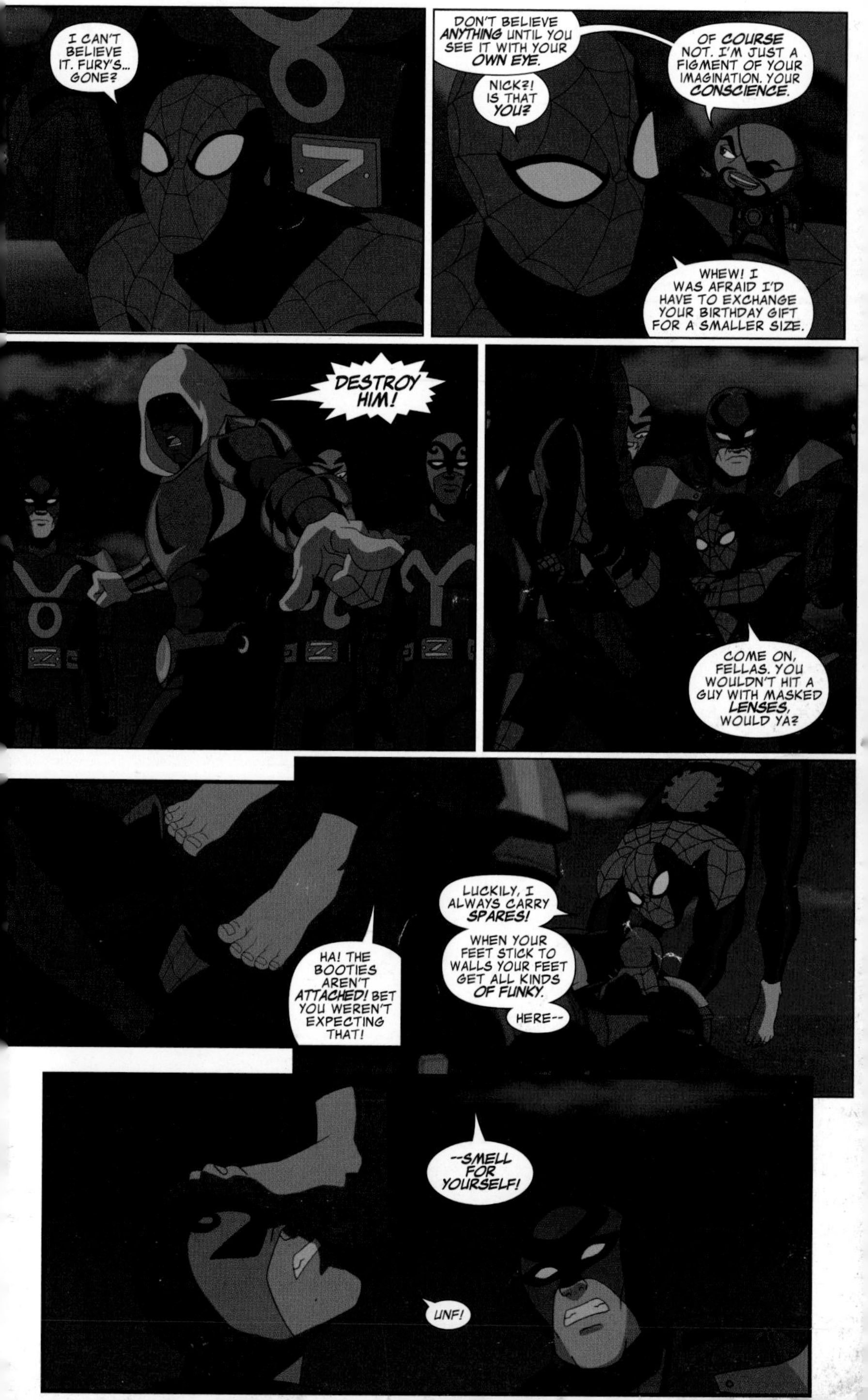

I CAN'T BELIEVE IT. FURY'S... GONE?
DON'T BELIEVE ANYTHING UNTIL YOU SEE IT WITH YOUR OWN EYE.
NICK?! IS THAT YOU?
OF COURSE NOT. I'M JUST A FIGMENT OF YOUR IMAGINATION. YOUR CONSCIENCE.
WHEW! I WAS AFRAID I'D HAVE TO EXCHANGE YOUR BIRTHDAY GIFT FOR A SMALLER SIZE.
DESTROY HIM!
COME ON, FELLAS. YOU WOULDN'T HIT A GUY WITH MASKED LENSES, WOULD YA?
HA! THE BOOTIES AREN'T ATTACHED! BET YOU WEREN'T EXPECTING THAT!
LUCKILY, I ALWAYS CARRY SPARES!
WHEN YOUR FEET STICK TO WALLS YOUR FEET GET ALL KINDS OF FUNKY.
HERE--
--SMELL FOR YOURSELF!
UNF!

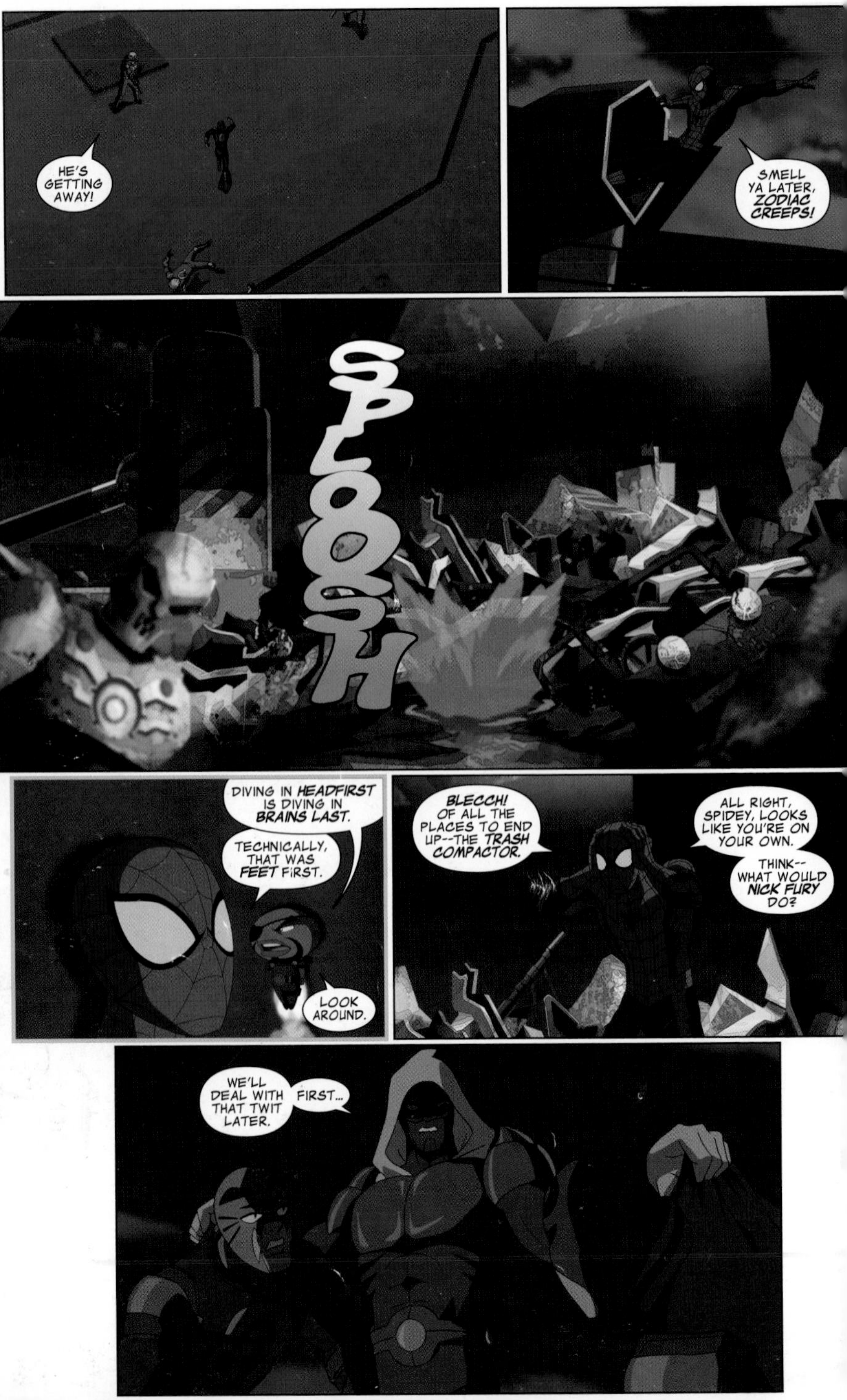

HE'S GETTING AWAY!
SMELL YA LATER, ZODIAC CREEPS!
SPLOOSH
DIVING IN HEADFIRST IS DIVING IN BRAINS LAST.
TECHNICALLY, THAT WAS FEET FIRST.
LOOK AROUND.
BLECCH! OF ALL THE PLACES TO END UP--THE TRASH COMPACTOR.
ALL RIGHT, SPIDEY, LOOKS LIKE YOU'RE ON YOUR OWN.
THINK-- WHAT WOULD NICK FURY DO?
WE'LL DEAL WITH THAT TWIT LATER.
FIRST...

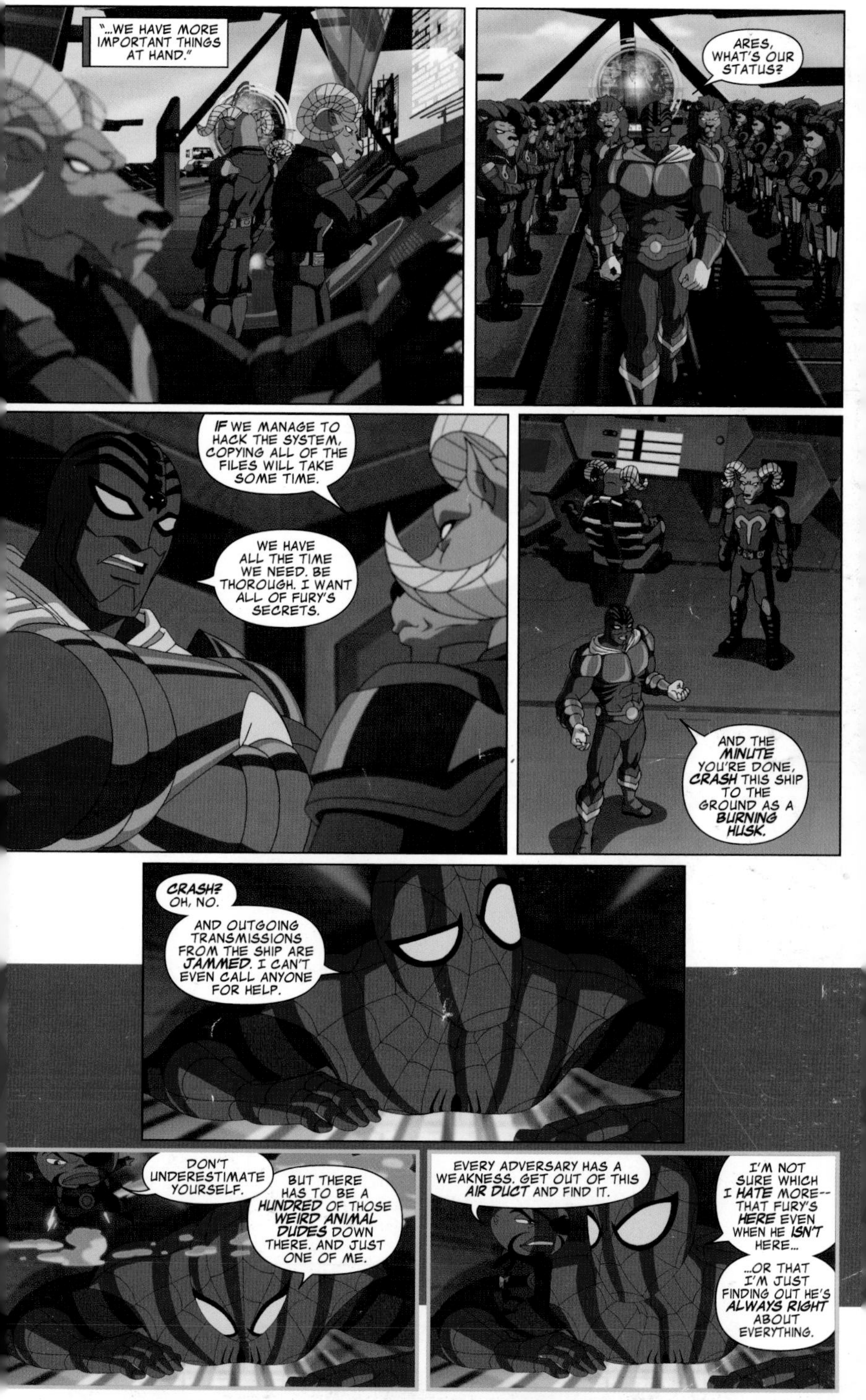
"...WE HAVE MORE IMPORTANT THINGS AT HAND."
ARES, WHAT'S OUR STATUS?
IF WE MANAGE TO HACK THE SYSTEM, COPYING ALL OF THE FILES WILL TAKE SOME TIME.
WE HAVE ALL THE TIME WE NEED. BE THOROUGH. I WANT ALL OF FURY'S SECRETS.
AND THE MINUTE YOU'RE DONE, CRASH THIS SHIP TO THE GROUND AS A BURNING HUSK.
CRASH? OH, NO.
AND OUTGOING TRANSMISSIONS FROM THE SHIP ARE JAMMED. I CAN'T EVEN CALL ANYONE FOR HELP.
DON'T UNDERESTIMATE YOURSELF.
BUT THERE HAS TO BE A HUNDRED OF THOSE WEIRD ANIMAL DUDES DOWN THERE. AND JUST ONE OF ME.
EVERY ADVERSARY HAS A WEAKNESS. GET OUT OF THIS AIR DUCT AND FIND IT.
I'M NOT SURE WHICH I HATE MORE-- THAT FURY'S HERE EVEN WHEN HE ISN'T HERE...
...OR THAT I'M JUST FINDING OUT HE'S ALWAYS RIGHT ABOUT EVERYTHING.

BUT HOW DO I FIND THEIR *WEAKNESS?* WHAT DO I *DO?*

KEEP IT TOGETHER, PARKER!

EXCUSE ME?

PLEASE, NO MORE *ADVICE,* LI'L NICK. I CAN'T HANDLE ANY MORE OF YOUR *WISDOM NUGGETS.*

HUH?!

FURY?! YOU'RE ALIVE?!

LISTEN--DO *NOT* ENGAGE ZODIAC ON YOUR OWN. THEY POSSESS THE *SCORPIO KEY.* IT'S ONE OF THE TEN MOST DANGEROUS WEAPONS KNOWN TO MAN.

THERE'S A *LIST* FOR THAT?

THERE'S A LIST FOR *EVERYTHING.*

IF WE DON'T GET THE SCORPIO KEY, ZODIAC CAN *RIP* THE S.H.I.E.L.D. HELICARRIER APART.

COME GET ME.

WHERE *ARE* YOU?

"MEDICAL BAY. SEVENTH LEVEL."

I'M TELLING YOU, I *HEARD* SOMEONE DOWN HERE.

IT COULD BE THAT SPIDER-MAN CREEP.

LET'S *SPLIT UP.* I'LL TAKE THE CORRIDOR TO THE LEFT, YOU GUYS GO RIGHT.

HMF. WHO LEFT *YOU* IN CHARGE ANYWAY?

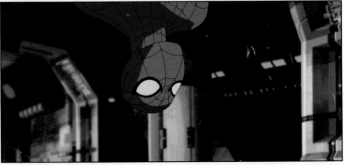

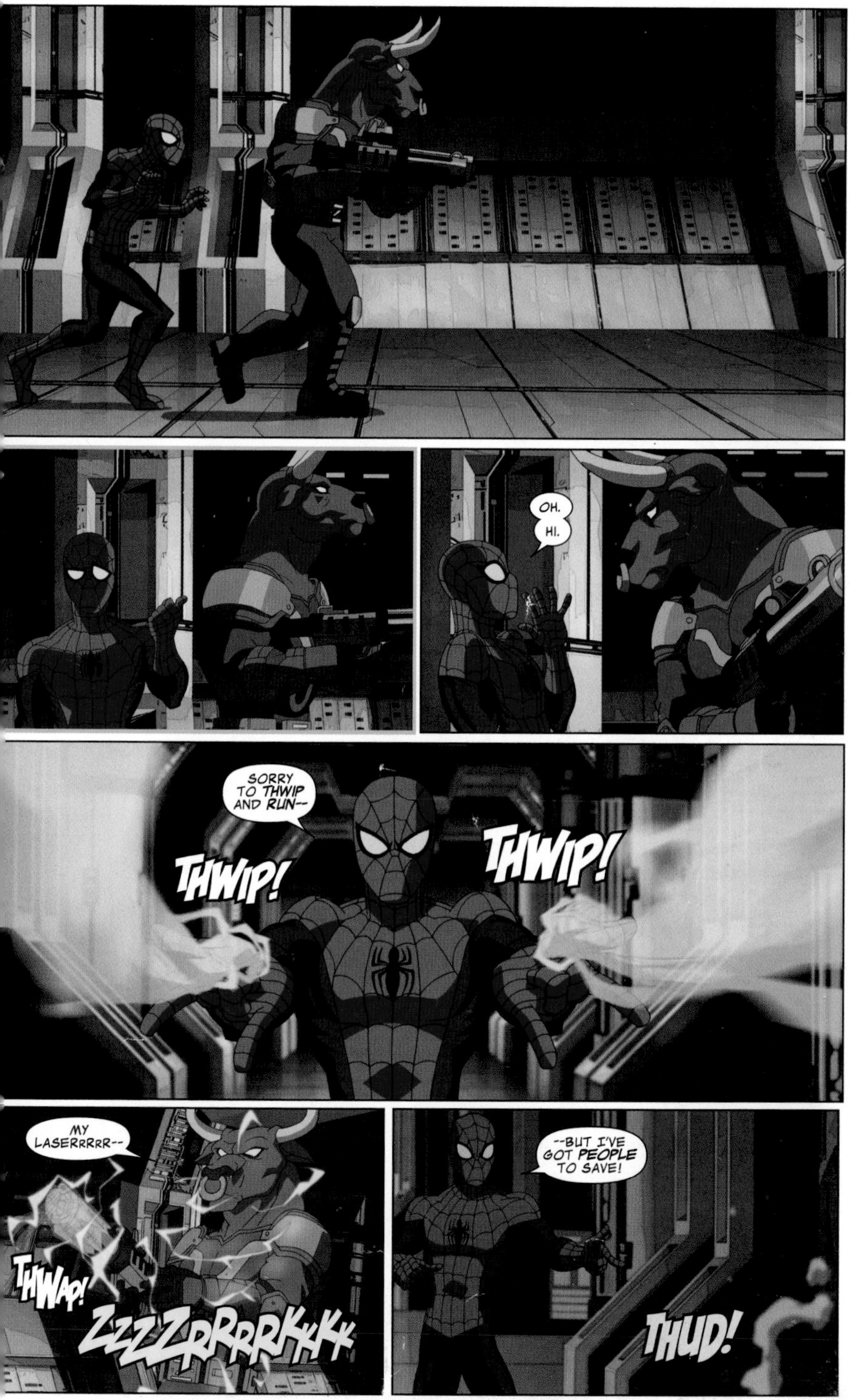
OH.
HI.
SORRY TO THWIP AND RUN--
THWIP!
THWIP!
MY LASERRRRR--
THWAP!
ZZZZRRRRRKKKK
--BUT I'VE GOT PEOPLE TO SAVE!
THUD!

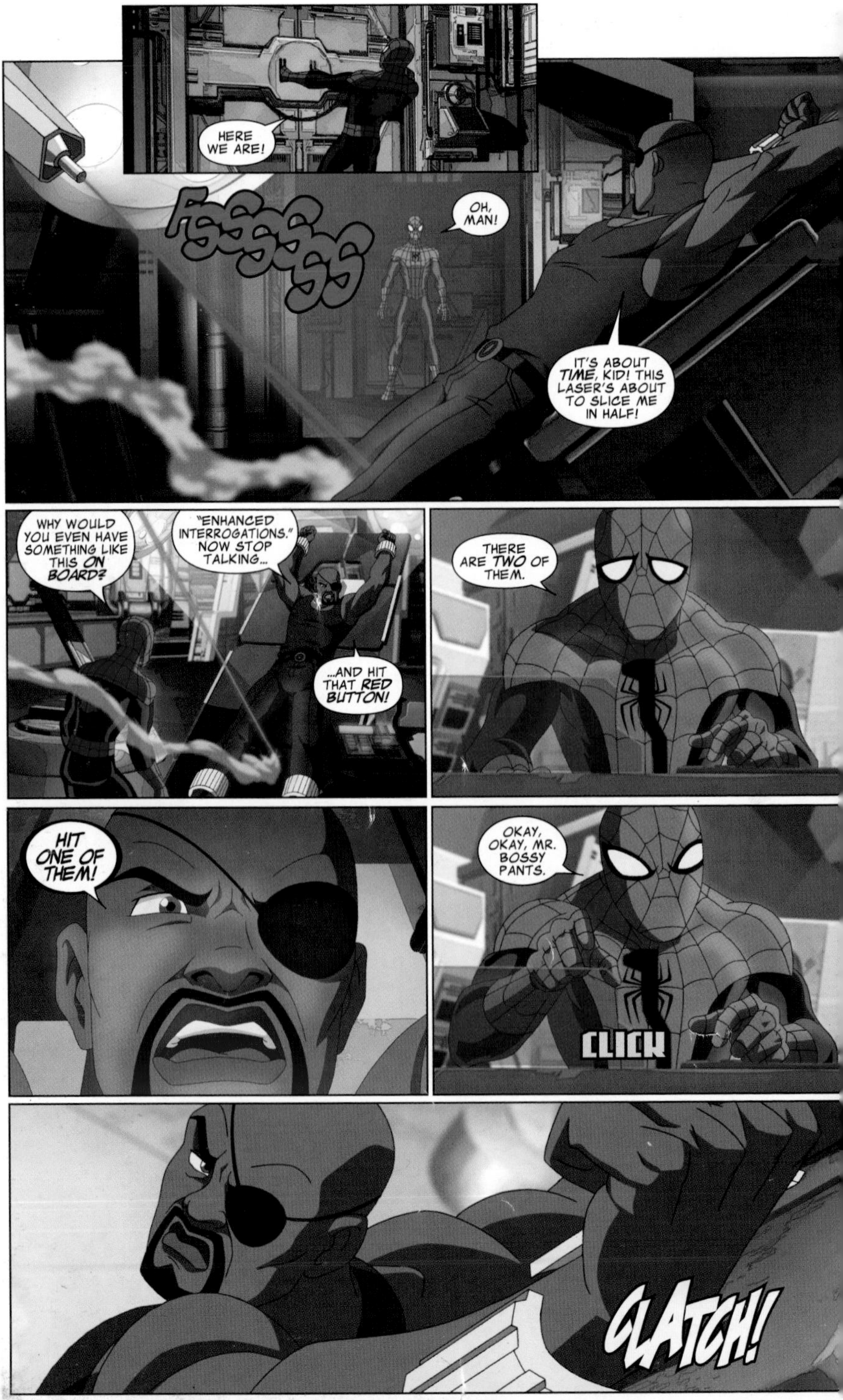

HERE WE ARE!
FSSSSSSS
OH, MAN!
IT'S ABOUT TIME, KID! THIS LASER'S ABOUT TO SLICE ME IN HALF!
WHY WOULD YOU EVEN HAVE SOMETHING LIKE THIS ON BOARD?
"ENHANCED INTERROGATIONS." NOW STOP TALKING...
...AND HIT THAT RED BUTTON!
THERE ARE TWO OF THEM.
HIT ONE OF THEM!
OKAY, OKAY, MR. BOSSY PANTS.
CLICK
CLATCH!

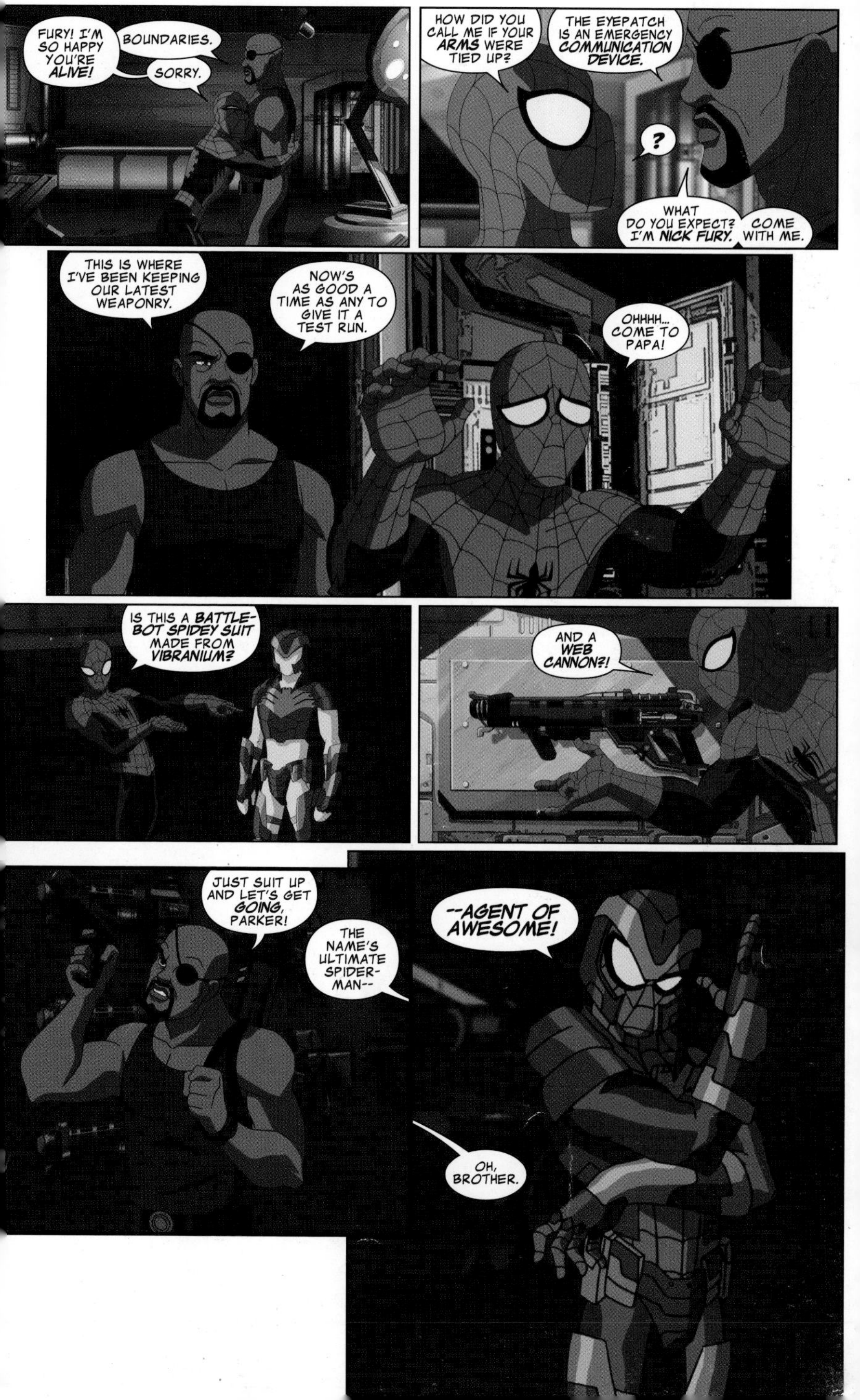
FURY! I'M SO HAPPY YOU'RE ALIVE!
BOUNDARIES.
SORRY.
HOW DID YOU CALL ME IF YOUR ARMS WERE TIED UP?
THE EYEPATCH IS AN EMERGENCY COMMUNICATION DEVICE.
?
WHAT DO YOU EXPECT? I'M NICK FURY.
COME WITH ME.
THIS IS WHERE I'VE BEEN KEEPING OUR LATEST WEAPONRY.
NOW'S AS GOOD A TIME AS ANY TO GIVE IT A TEST RUN.
OHHHH... COME TO PAPA!
IS THIS A BATTLE-BOT SPIDEY SUIT MADE FROM VIBRANIUM?
AND A WEB CANNON?!
JUST SUIT UP AND LET'S GET GOING, PARKER!
THE NAME'S ULTIMATE SPIDER-MAN--
--AGENT OF AWESOME!
OH, BROTHER.

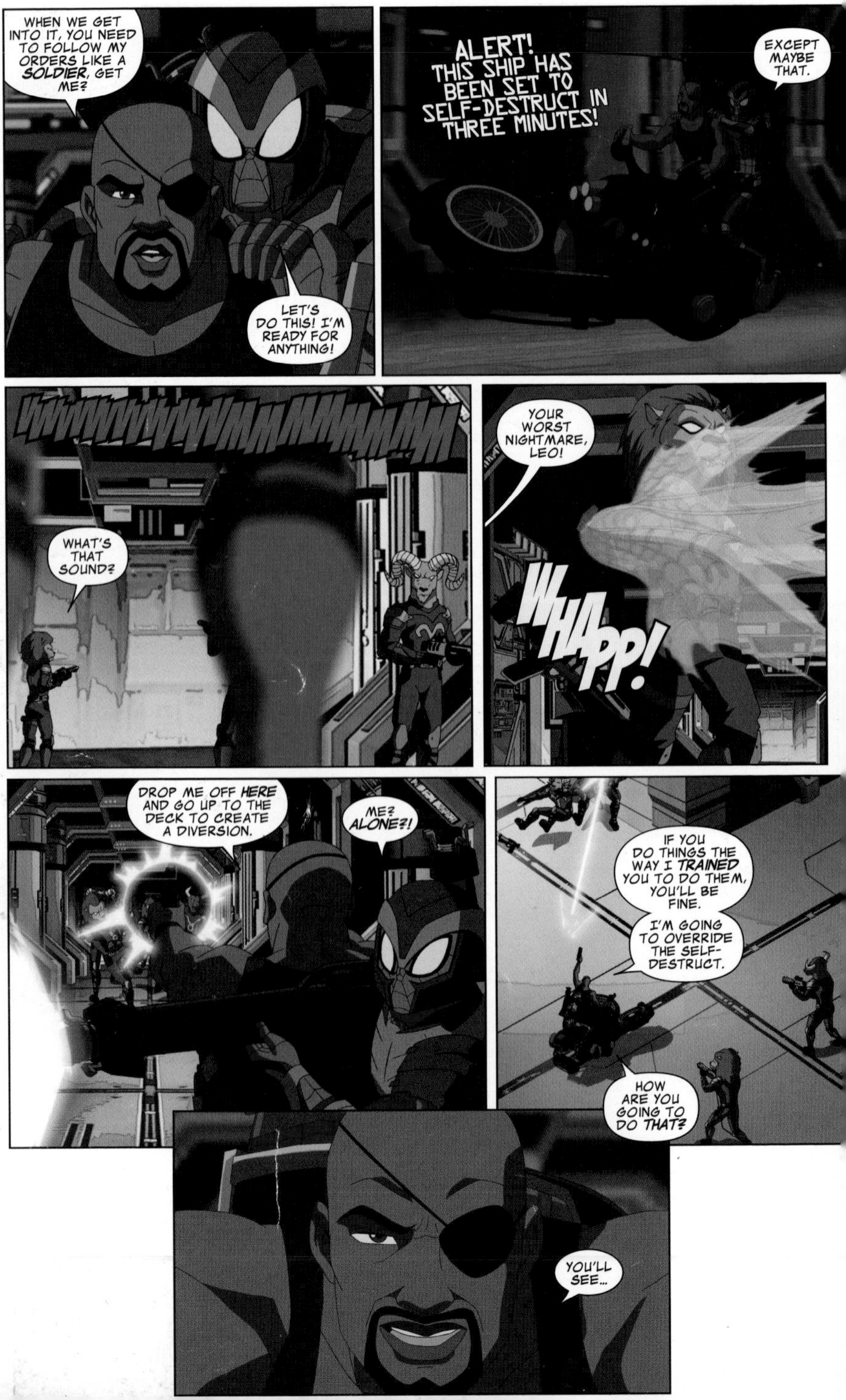
WHEN WE GET INTO IT, YOU NEED TO FOLLOW MY ORDERS LIKE A SOLDIER, GET ME?
LET'S DO THIS! I'M READY FOR ANYTHING!
ALERT! THIS SHIP HAS BEEN SET TO SELF-DESTRUCT IN THREE MINUTES!
EXCEPT MAYBE THAT.
VWVWVWVWVWVMMMMMMMM
WHAT'S THAT SOUND?
YOUR WORST NIGHTMARE, LEO!
WHAPP!
DROP ME OFF HERE AND GO UP TO THE DECK TO CREATE A DIVERSION.
ME? ALONE?!
IF YOU DO THINGS THE WAY I TRAINED YOU TO DO THEM, YOU'LL BE FINE.
I'M GOING TO OVERRIDE THE SELF-DESTRUCT.
HOW ARE YOU GOING TO DO THAT?
YOU'LL SEE...

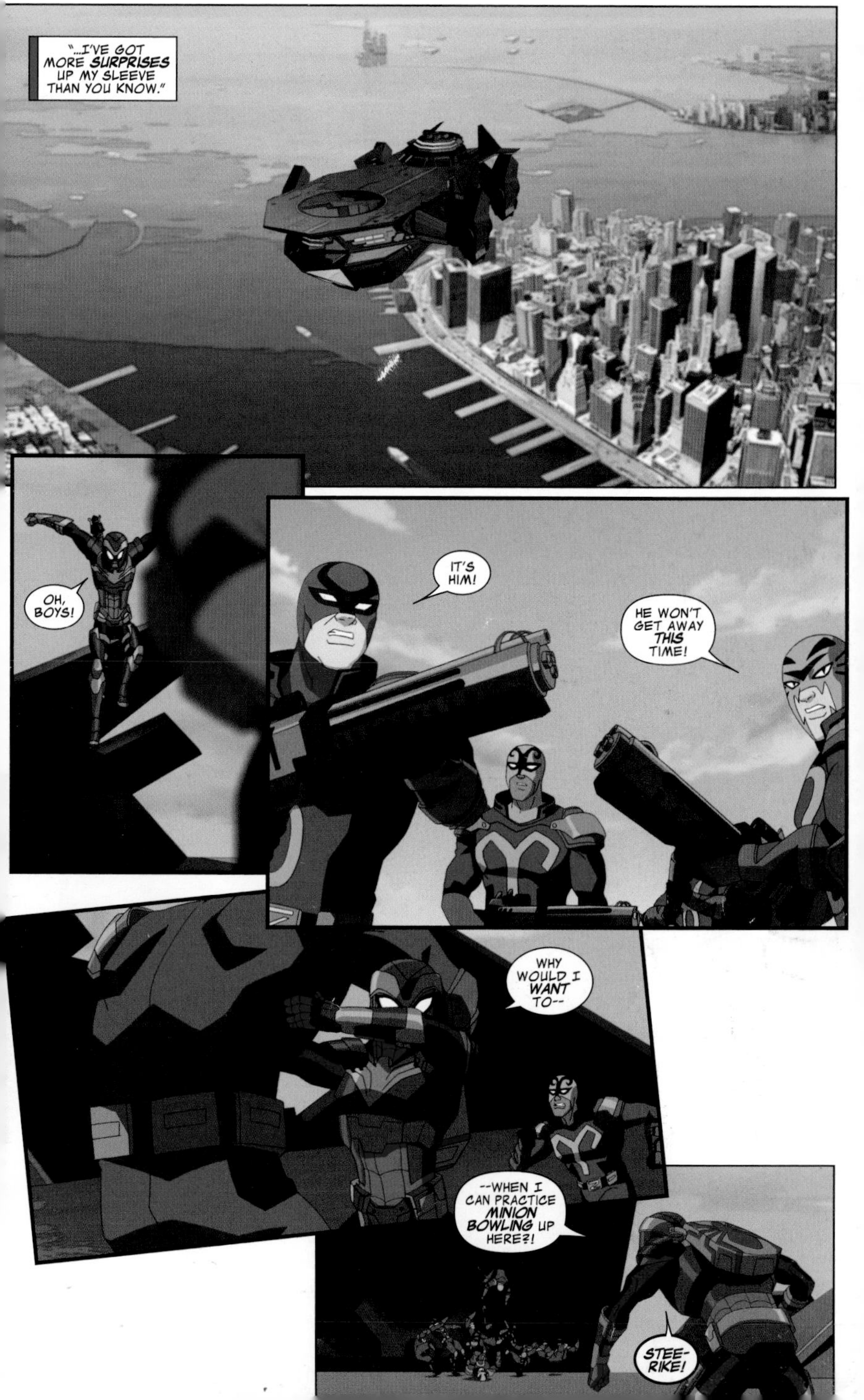
"...I'VE GOT MORE SURPRISES UP MY SLEEVE THAN YOU KNOW."
OH, BOYS!
IT'S HIM!
HE WON'T GET AWAY THIS TIME!
WHY WOULD I WANT TO--
--WHEN I CAN PRACTICE MINION BOWLING UP HERE?!
STEE-RIKE!

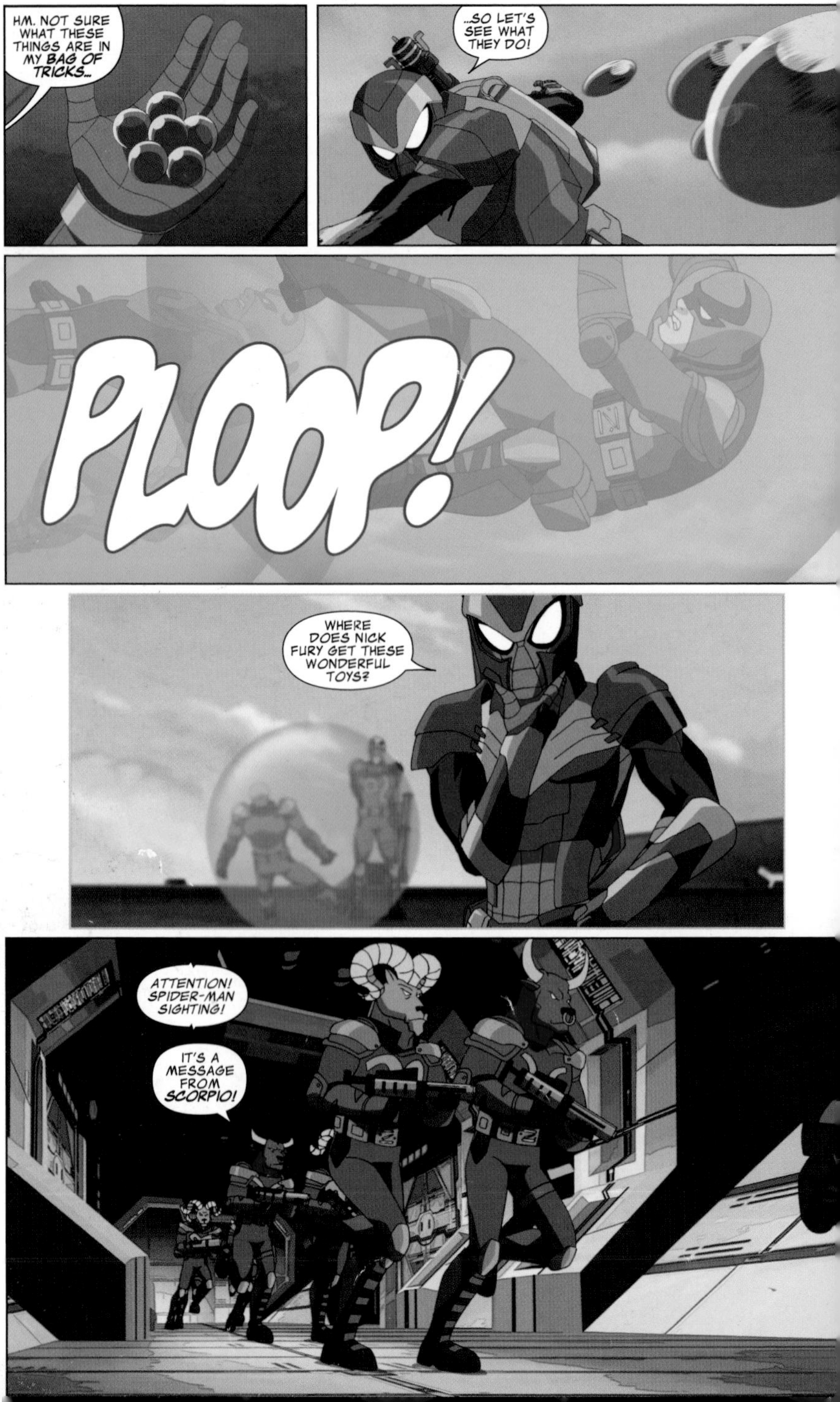
HM. NOT SURE WHAT THESE THINGS ARE IN MY BAG OF TRICKS...
...SO LET'S SEE WHAT THEY DO!
PLOOP!
WHERE DOES NICK FURY GET THESE WONDERFUL TOYS?
ATTENTION! SPIDER-MAN SIGHTING!
IT'S A MESSAGE FROM SCORPIO!

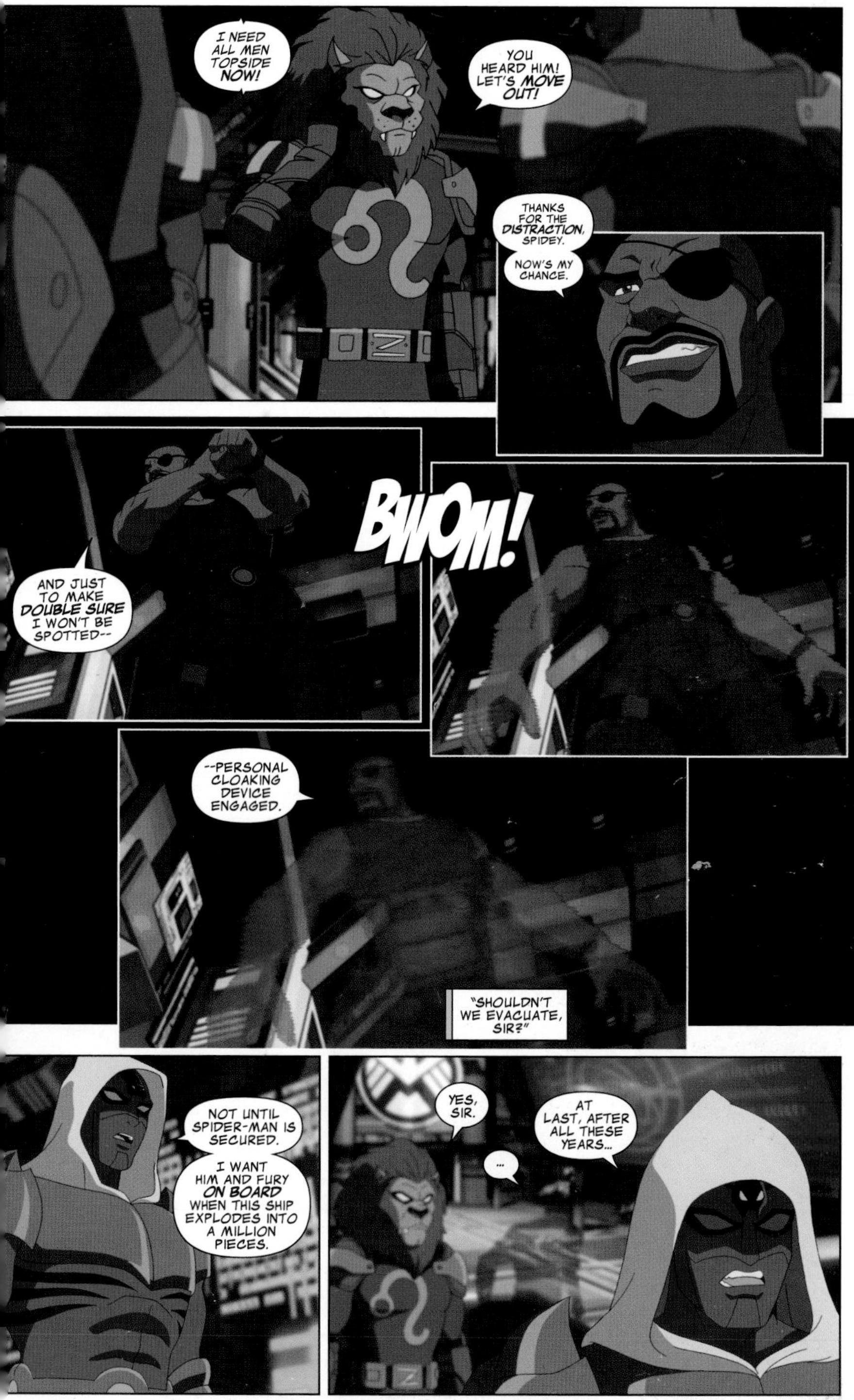
I NEED ALL MEN TOPSIDE NOW!
YOU HEARD HIM! LET'S MOVE OUT!
THANKS FOR THE DISTRACTION, SPIDEY.
NOW'S MY CHANCE.
AND JUST TO MAKE DOUBLE SURE I WON'T BE SPOTTED--
BWOM!
--PERSONAL CLOAKING DEVICE ENGAGED.
"SHOULDN'T WE EVACUATE, SIR?"
NOT UNTIL SPIDER-MAN IS SECURED.
I WANT HIM AND FURY ON BOARD WHEN THIS SHIP EXPLODES INTO A MILLION PIECES.
YES, SIR.
...
AT LAST, AFTER ALL THESE YEARS...

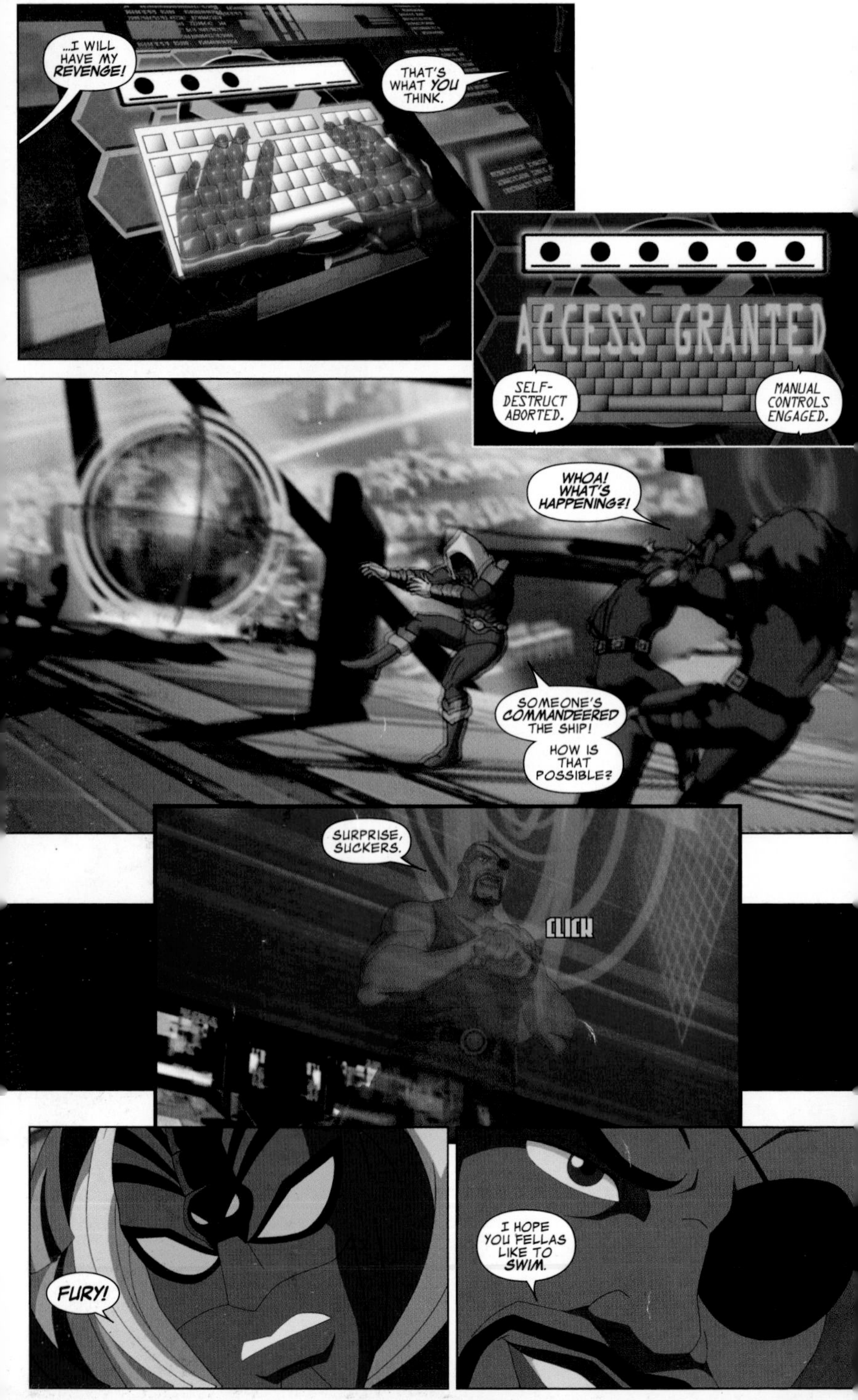

...I WILL HAVE MY REVENGE!
THAT'S WHAT YOU THINK.
ACCESS GRANTED
SELF-DESTRUCT ABORTED.
MANUAL CONTROLS ENGAGED.
WHOA! WHAT'S HAPPENING?!
SOMEONE'S COMMANDEERED THE SHIP!
HOW IS THAT POSSIBLE?
SURPRISE, SUCKERS.
CLICK
FURY!
I HOPE YOU FELLAS LIKE TO SWIM.

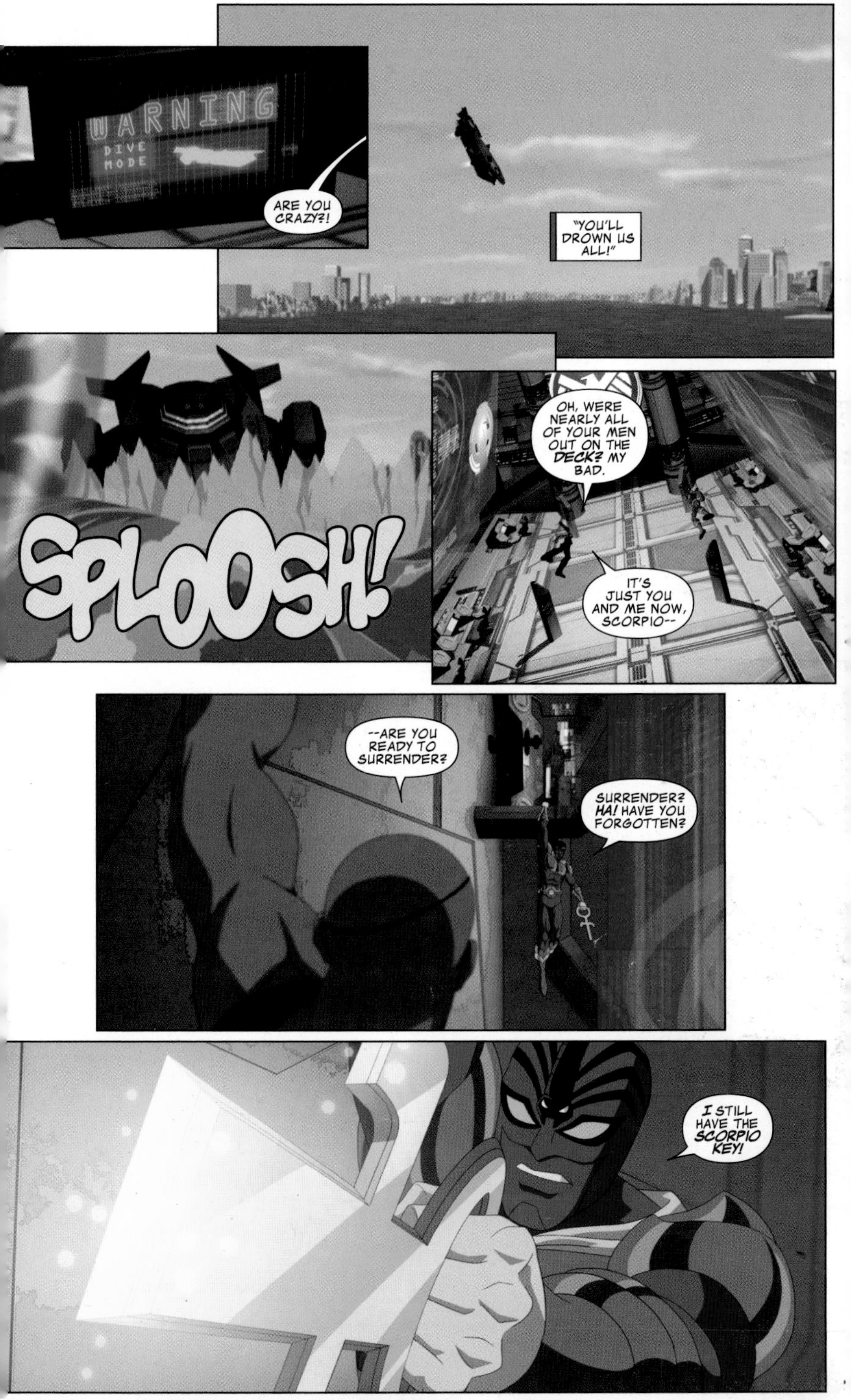
WARNING
DIVE MODE
ARE YOU CRAZY?!
"YOU'LL DROWN US ALL!"
SPLOOSH!
OH, WERE NEARLY ALL OF YOUR MEN OUT ON THE DECK? MY BAD.
IT'S JUST YOU AND ME NOW, SCORPIO--
--ARE YOU READY TO SURRENDER?
SURRENDER? HA! HAVE YOU FORGOTTEN?
I STILL HAVE THE SCORPIO KEY!

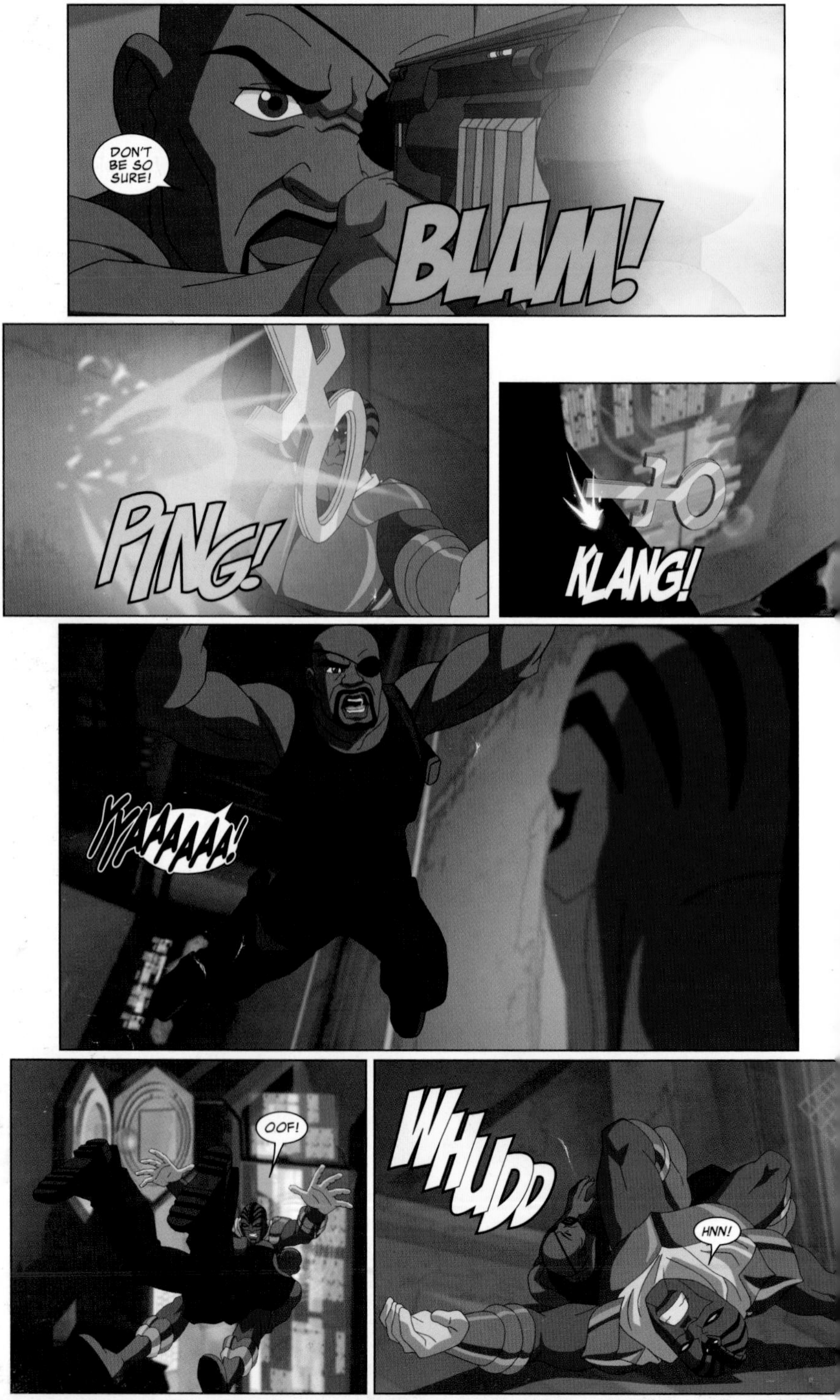

DON'T BE SO SURE!
BLAM!
PING!
KLANG!
YYAAAAAA!
OOF!
WHUDD
HNN!

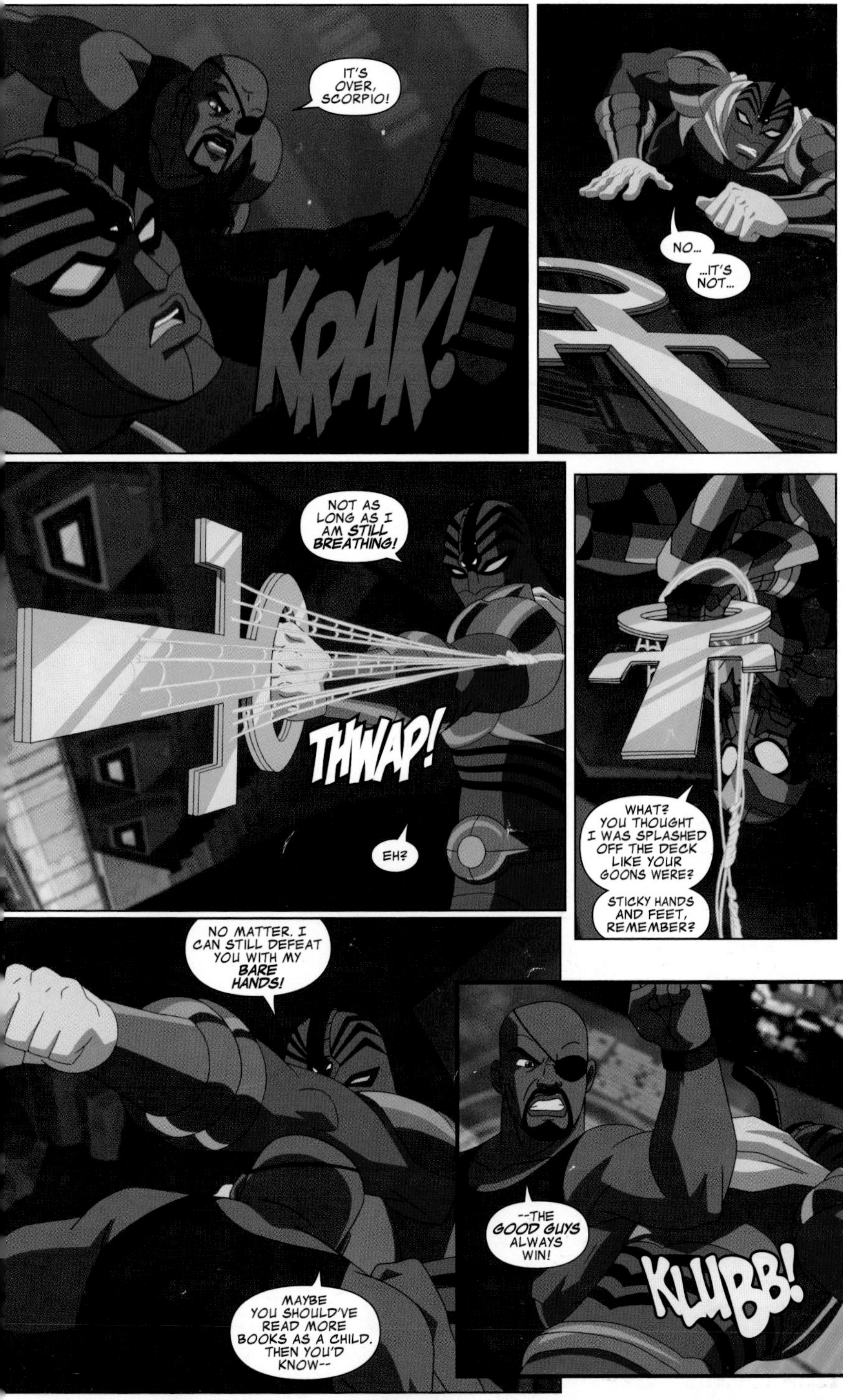
IT'S OVER, SCORPIO!
KRAK!
NO... ...IT'S NOT...
NOT AS LONG AS I AM STILL BREATHING!
THWAP!
EH?
WHAT? YOU THOUGHT I WAS SPLASHED OFF THE DECK LIKE YOUR GOONS WERE?
STICKY HANDS AND FEET, REMEMBER?
NO MATTER. I CAN STILL DEFEAT YOU WITH MY BARE HANDS!
MAYBE YOU SHOULD'VE READ MORE BOOKS AS A CHILD. THEN YOU'D KNOW--
--THE GOOD GUYS ALWAYS WIN!
KLUBB!

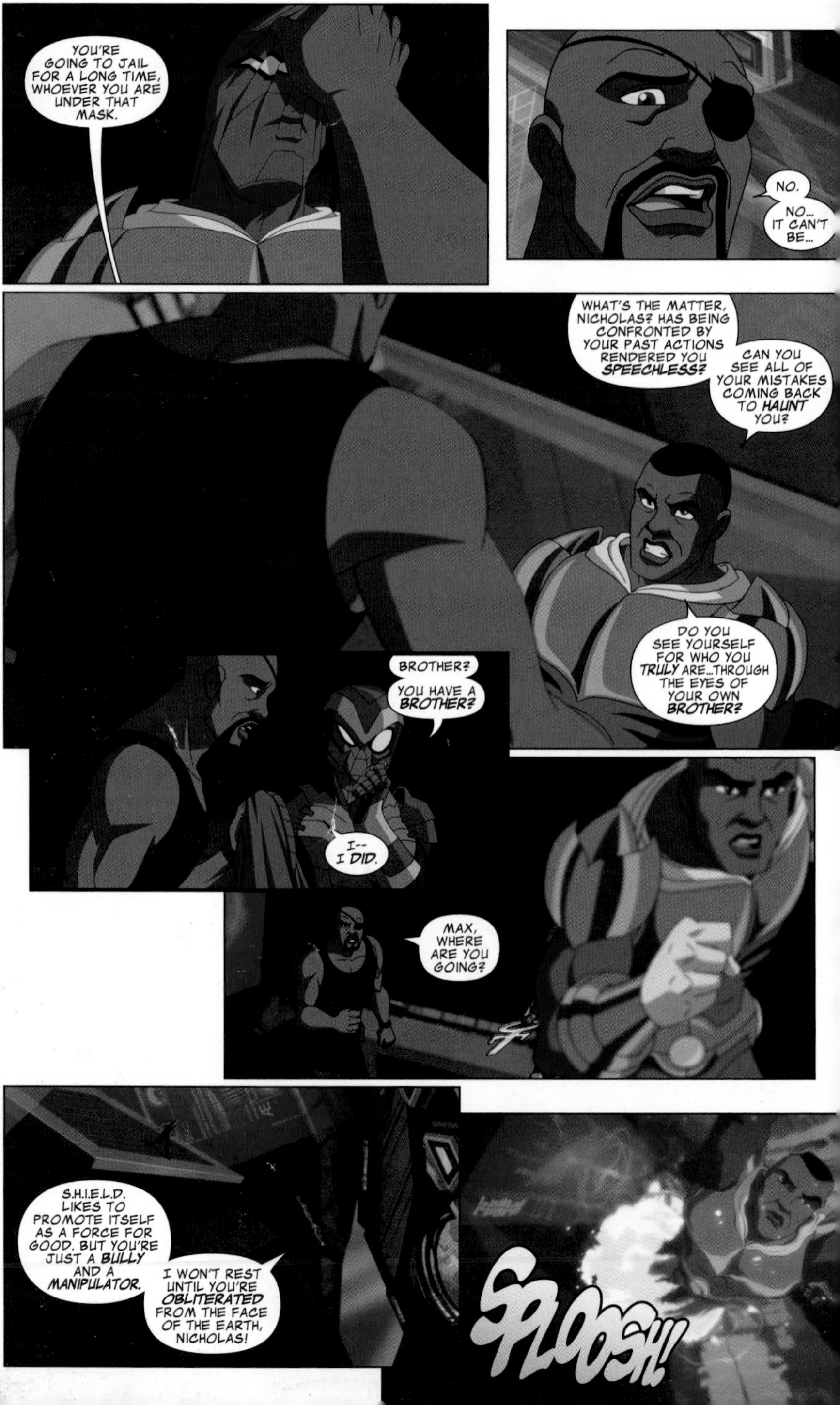

YOU'RE GOING TO JAIL FOR A LONG TIME, WHOEVER YOU ARE UNDER THAT MASK.
NO.
NO... IT CAN'T BE...
WHAT'S THE MATTER, NICHOLAS? HAS BEING CONFRONTED BY YOUR PAST ACTIONS RENDERED YOU SPEECHLESS?
CAN YOU SEE ALL OF YOUR MISTAKES COMING BACK TO HAUNT YOU?
DO YOU SEE YOURSELF FOR WHO YOU TRULY ARE...THROUGH THE EYES OF YOUR OWN BROTHER?
BROTHER?
YOU HAVE A BROTHER?
I-- I DID.
MAX, WHERE ARE YOU GOING?
S.H.I.E.L.D. LIKES TO PROMOTE ITSELF AS A FORCE FOR GOOD. BUT YOU'RE JUST A BULLY AND A MANIPULATOR.
I WON'T REST UNTIL YOU'RE OBLITERATED FROM THE FACE OF THE EARTH, NICHOLAS!
SPLOOSH!

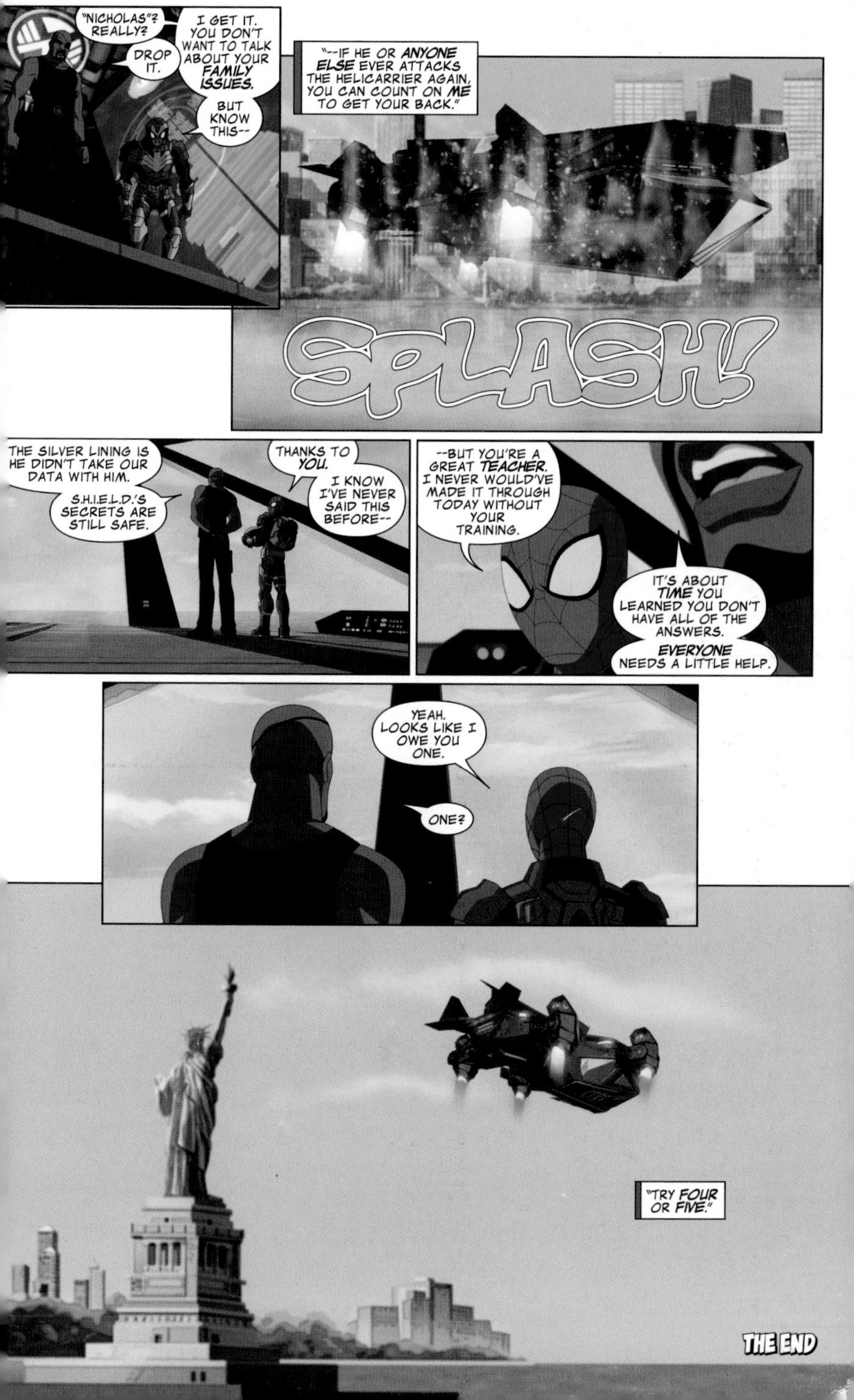
"NICHOLAS"? REALLY?
I GET IT. YOU DON'T WANT TO TALK ABOUT YOUR FAMILY ISSUES.
DROP IT.
BUT KNOW THIS--
"--IF HE OR ANYONE ELSE EVER ATTACKS THE HELICARRIER AGAIN, YOU CAN COUNT ON ME TO GET YOUR BACK."
SPLASH!
THE SILVER LINING IS HE DIDN'T TAKE OUR DATA WITH HIM.
S.H.I.E.L.D.'S SECRETS ARE STILL SAFE.
THANKS TO YOU.
I KNOW I'VE NEVER SAID THIS BEFORE--
--BUT YOU'RE A GREAT TEACHER. I NEVER WOULD'VE MADE IT THROUGH TODAY WITHOUT YOUR TRAINING.
IT'S ABOUT TIME YOU LEARNED YOU DON'T HAVE ALL OF THE ANSWERS.
EVERYONE NEEDS A LITTLE HELP.
YEAH. LOOKS LIKE I OWE YOU ONE.
ONE?
"TRY FOUR OR FIVE."
THE END

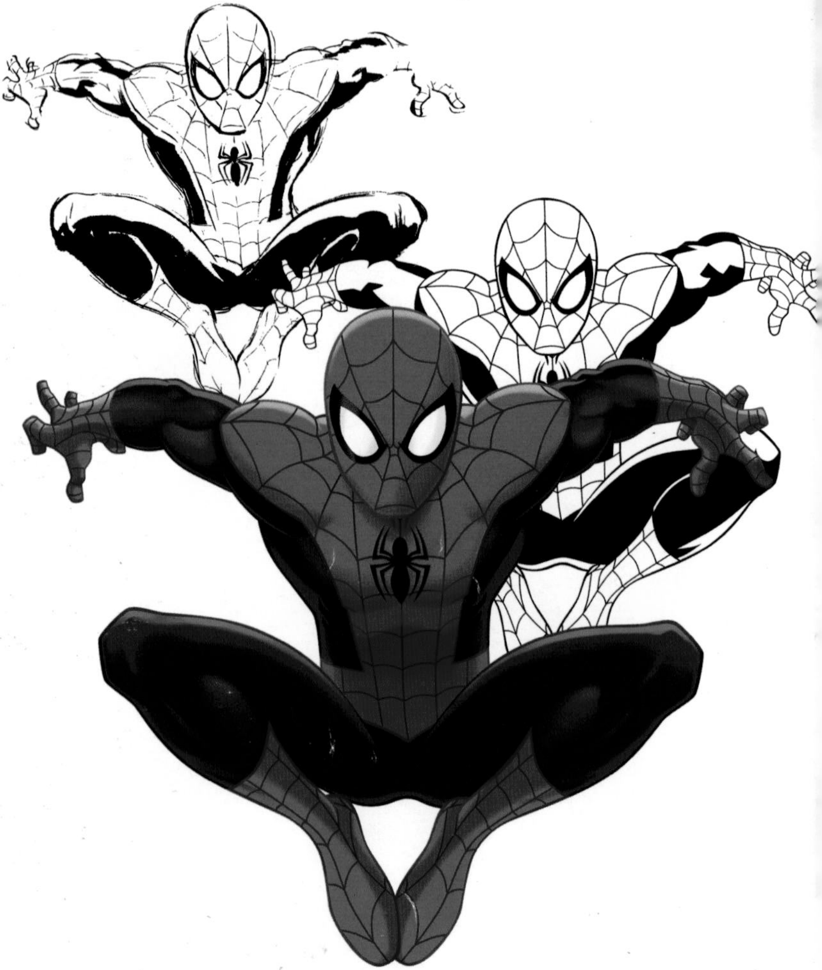

Based on "Beetle Mania"

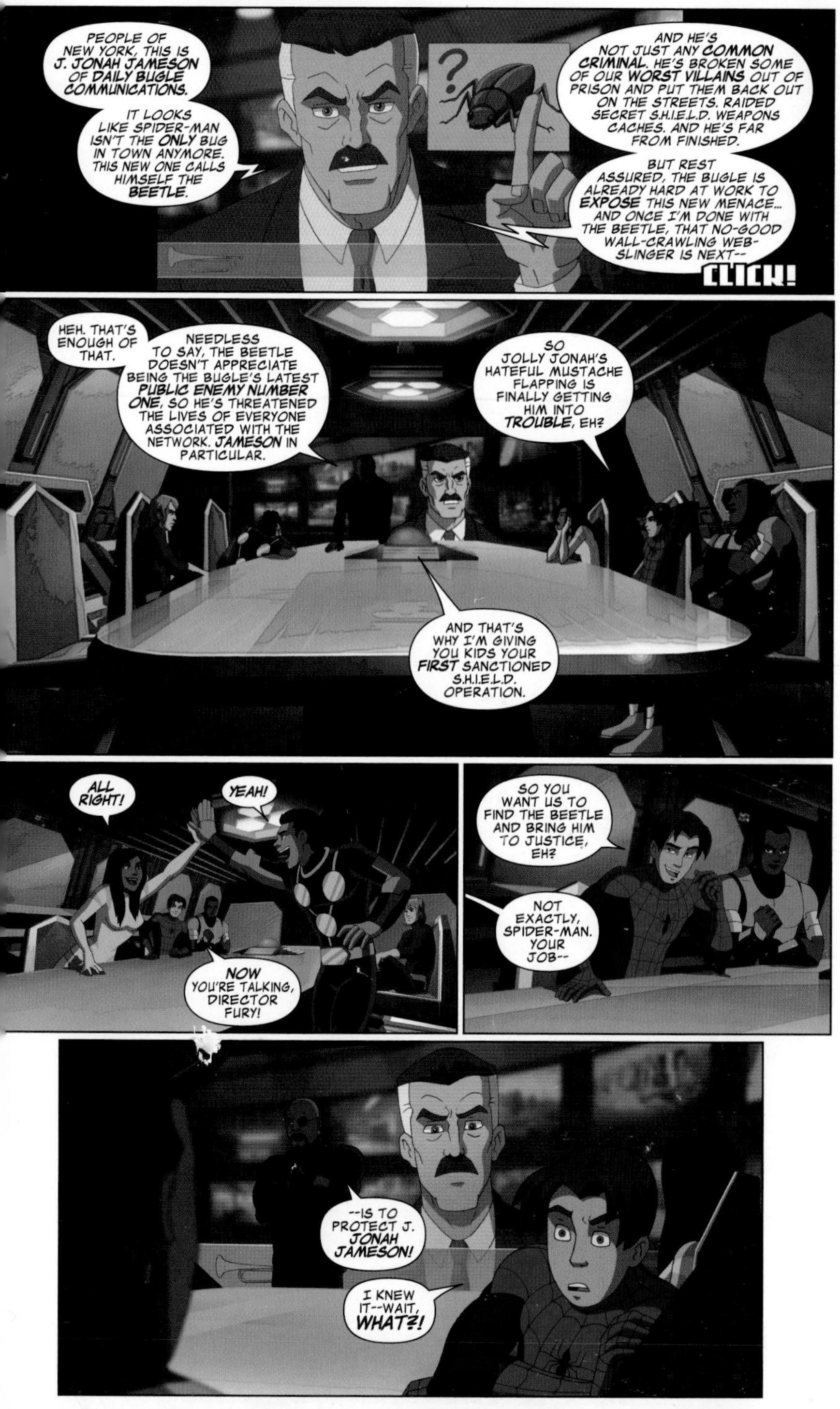
PEOPLE OF NEW YORK, THIS IS J. JONAH JAMESON OF DAILY BUGLE COMMUNICATIONS.
IT LOOKS LIKE SPIDER-MAN ISN'T THE ONLY BUG IN TOWN ANYMORE. THIS NEW ONE CALLS HIMSELF THE BEETLE.
?
AND HE'S NOT JUST ANY COMMON CRIMINAL. HE'S BROKEN SOME OF OUR WORST VILLAINS OUT OF PRISON AND PUT THEM BACK OUT ON THE STREETS. RAIDED SECRET S.H.I.E.L.D. WEAPONS CACHES. AND HE'S FAR FROM FINISHED.
BUT REST ASSURED, THE BUGLE IS ALREADY HARD AT WORK TO EXPOSE THIS NEW MENACE... AND ONCE I'M DONE WITH THE BEETLE, THAT NO-GOOD WALL-CRAWLING WEB-SLINGER IS NEXT--
CLICK!
HEH. THAT'S ENOUGH OF THAT.
NEEDLESS TO SAY, THE BEETLE DOESN'T APPRECIATE BEING THE BUGLE'S LATEST PUBLIC ENEMY NUMBER ONE, SO HE'S THREATENED THE LIVES OF EVERYONE ASSOCIATED WITH THE NETWORK. JAMESON IN PARTICULAR.
SO JOLLY JONAH'S HATEFUL MUSTACHE FLAPPING IS FINALLY GETTING HIM INTO TROUBLE, EH?
AND THAT'S WHY I'M GIVING YOU KIDS YOUR FIRST SANCTIONED S.H.I.E.L.D. OPERATION.
ALL RIGHT!
YEAH!
NOW YOU'RE TALKING, DIRECTOR FURY!
SO YOU WANT US TO FIND THE BEETLE AND BRING HIM TO JUSTICE, EH?
NOT EXACTLY, SPIDER-MAN. YOUR JOB--
--IS TO PROTECT J. JONAH JAMESON!
I KNEW IT--WAIT, WHAT?!

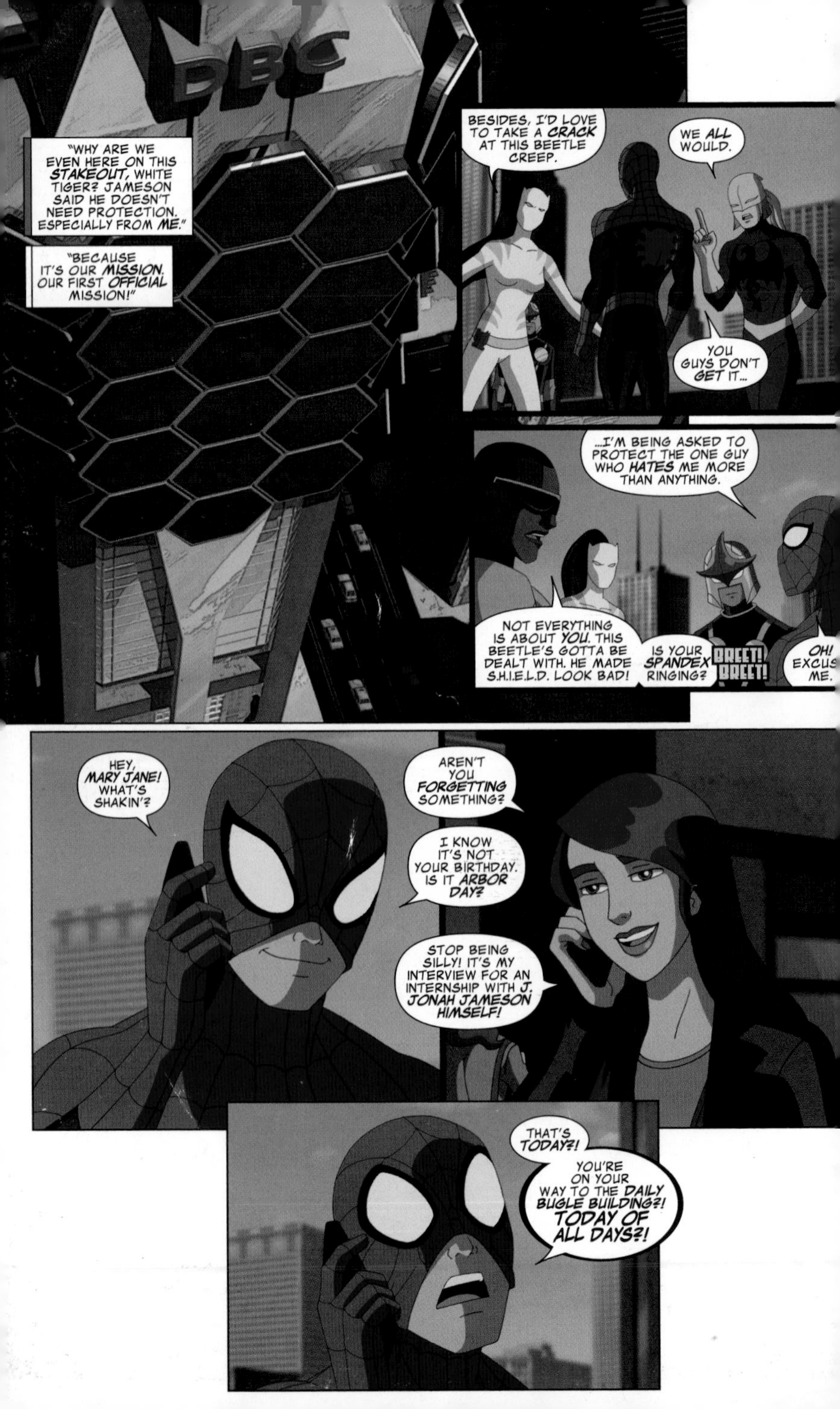

DBC
"WHY ARE WE EVEN HERE ON THIS STAKEOUT, WHITE TIGER? JAMESON SAID HE DOESN'T NEED PROTECTION. ESPECIALLY FROM ME."
"BECAUSE IT'S OUR MISSION. OUR FIRST OFFICIAL MISSION!"
BESIDES, I'D LOVE TO TAKE A CRACK AT THIS BEETLE CREEP.
WE ALL WOULD.
YOU GUYS DON'T GET IT...
...I'M BEING ASKED TO PROTECT THE ONE GUY WHO HATES ME MORE THAN ANYTHING.
NOT EVERYTHING IS ABOUT YOU. THIS BEETLE'S GOTTA BE DEALT WITH. HE MADE S.H.I.E.L.D. LOOK BAD!
IS YOUR SPANDEX RINGING?
BREET! BREET!
OH! EXCUS ME.
HEY, MARY JANE! WHAT'S SHAKIN'?
AREN'T YOU FORGETTING SOMETHING?
I KNOW IT'S NOT YOUR BIRTHDAY. IS IT ARBOR DAY?
STOP BEING SILLY! IT'S MY INTERVIEW FOR AN INTERNSHIP WITH J. JONAH JAMESON HIMSELF!
THAT'S TODAY?!
YOU'RE ON YOUR WAY TO THE DAILY BUGLE BUILDING?! TODAY OF ALL DAYS?!

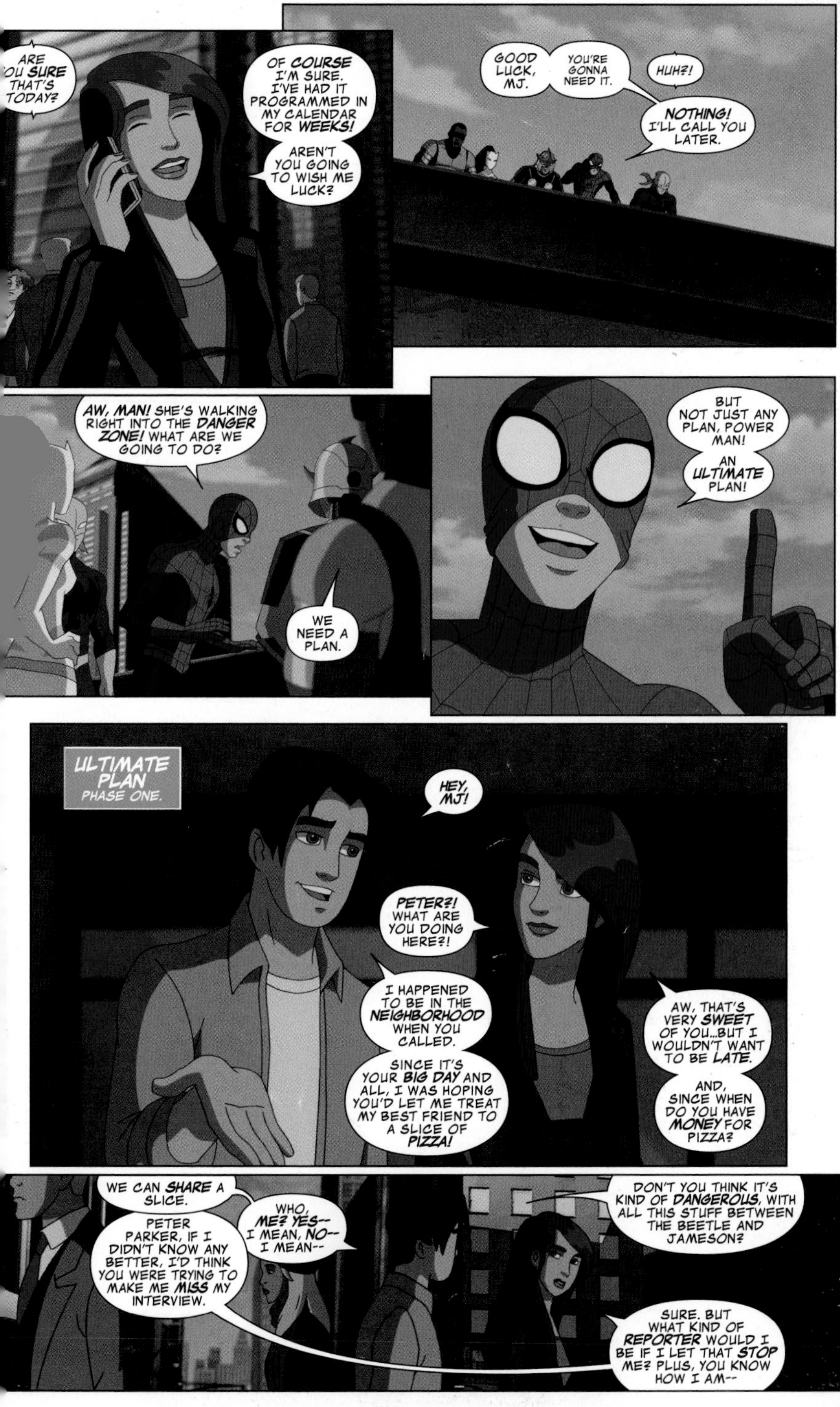
ARE YOU SURE THAT'S TODAY?
OF COURSE I'M SURE. I'VE HAD IT PROGRAMMED IN MY CALENDAR FOR WEEKS!
AREN'T YOU GOING TO WISH ME LUCK?
GOOD LUCK, MJ.
YOU'RE GONNA NEED IT.
HUH?!
NOTHING! I'LL CALL YOU LATER.
AW, MAN! SHE'S WALKING RIGHT INTO THE DANGER ZONE! WHAT ARE WE GOING TO DO?
WE NEED A PLAN.
BUT NOT JUST ANY PLAN, POWER MAN!
AN ULTIMATE PLAN!
ULTIMATE PLAN PHASE ONE.
HEY, MJ!
PETER?! WHAT ARE YOU DOING HERE?!
I HAPPENED TO BE IN THE NEIGHBORHOOD WHEN YOU CALLED.
SINCE IT'S YOUR BIG DAY AND ALL, I WAS HOPING YOU'D LET ME TREAT MY BEST FRIEND TO A SLICE OF PIZZA!
AW, THAT'S VERY SWEET OF YOU...BUT I WOULDN'T WANT TO BE LATE.
AND, SINCE WHEN DO YOU HAVE MONEY FOR PIZZA?
WE CAN SHARE A SLICE.
PETER PARKER, IF I DIDN'T KNOW ANY BETTER, I'D THINK YOU WERE TRYING TO MAKE ME MISS MY INTERVIEW.
WHO, ME? YES-- I MEAN, NO-- I MEAN--
DON'T YOU THINK IT'S KIND OF DANGEROUS, WITH ALL THIS STUFF BETWEEN THE BEETLE AND JAMESON?
SURE. BUT WHAT KIND OF REPORTER WOULD I BE IF I LET THAT STOP ME? PLUS, YOU KNOW HOW I AM--

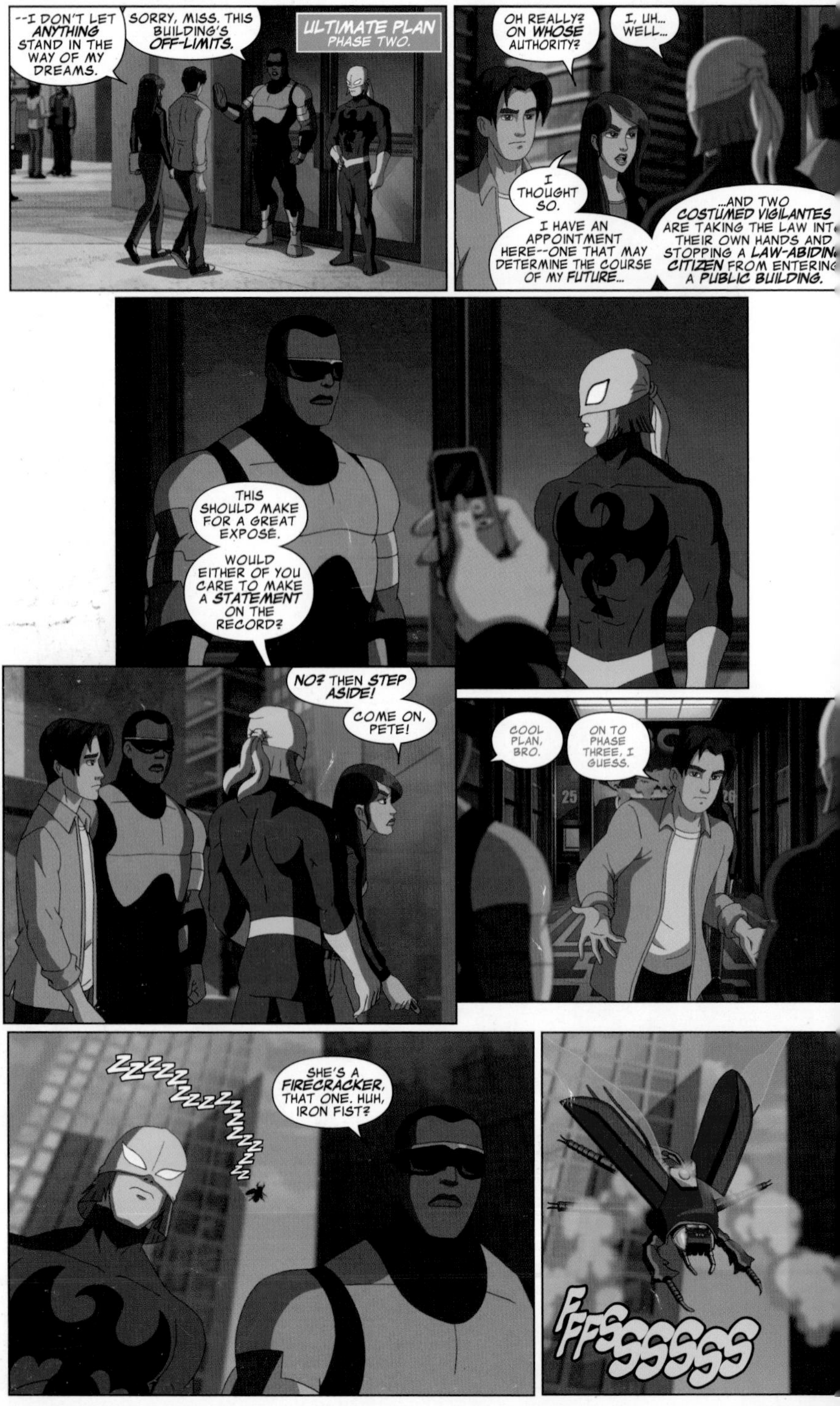

--I DON'T LET ANYTHING STAND IN THE WAY OF MY DREAMS.
SORRY, MISS. THIS BUILDING'S OFF-LIMITS.
ULTIMATE PLAN PHASE TWO.
OH REALLY? ON WHOSE AUTHORITY?
I, UH... WELL...
I THOUGHT SO.
I HAVE AN APPOINTMENT HERE--ONE THAT MAY DETERMINE THE COURSE OF MY FUTURE...
...AND TWO COSTUMED VIGILANTES ARE TAKING THE LAW INTO THEIR OWN HANDS AND STOPPING A LAW-ABIDING CITIZEN FROM ENTERING A PUBLIC BUILDING.
THIS SHOULD MAKE FOR A GREAT EXPOSE.
WOULD EITHER OF YOU CARE TO MAKE A STATEMENT ON THE RECORD?
NO? THEN STEP ASIDE!
COME ON, PETE!
COOL PLAN, BRO.
ON TO PHASE THREE, I GUESS.
ZZZZZZZZZZZZZZZZ
SHE'S A FIRECRACKER, THAT ONE. HUH, IRON FIST?
FFFSSSSSSS

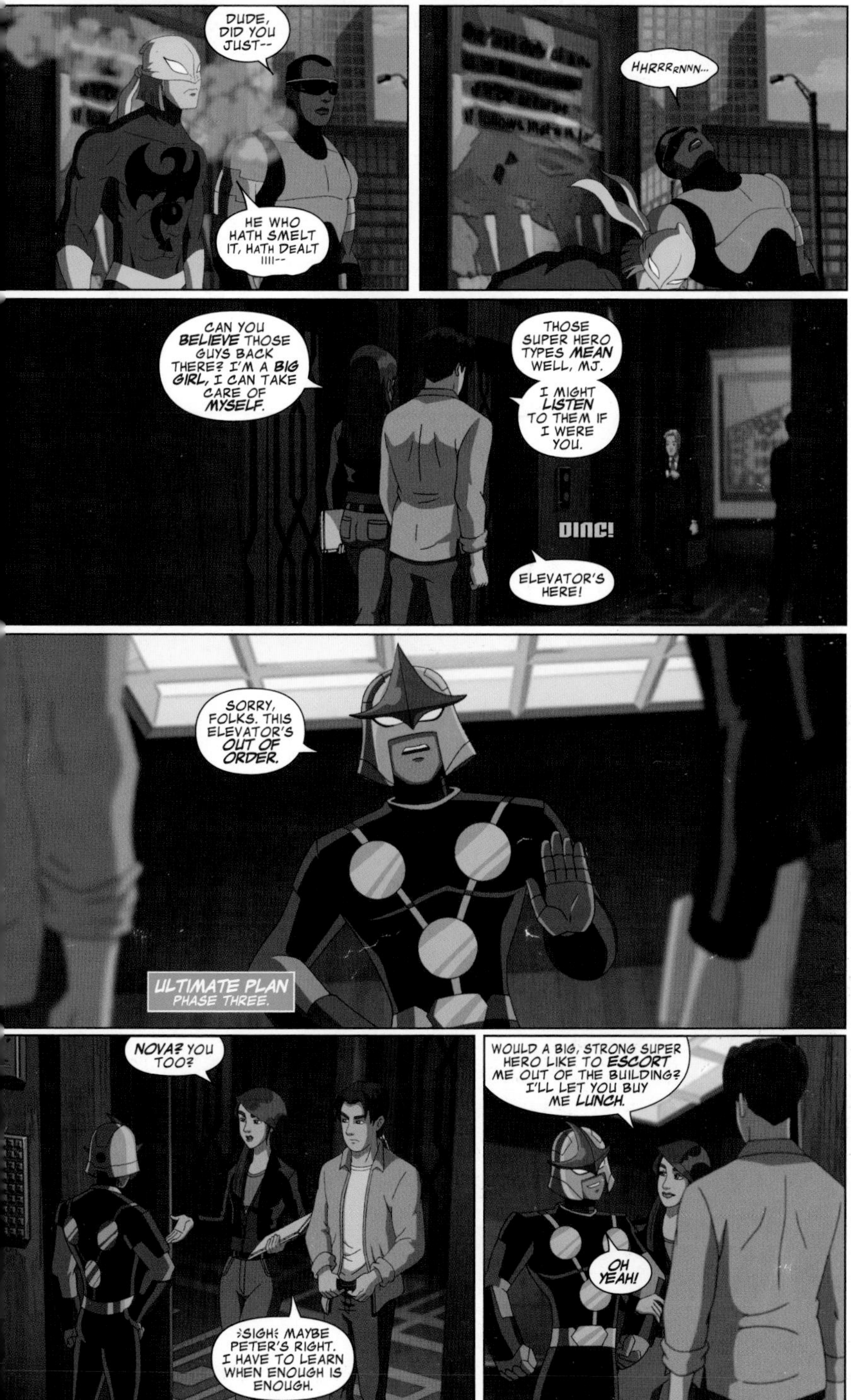
DUDE, DID YOU JUST--
HE WHO HATH SMELT IT, HATH DEALT IIII--
HHRRRRNNN...
CAN YOU BELIEVE THOSE GUYS BACK THERE? I'M A BIG GIRL, I CAN TAKE CARE OF MYSELF.
THOSE SUPER HERO TYPES MEAN WELL, MJ.
I MIGHT LISTEN TO THEM IF I WERE YOU.
DING!
ELEVATOR'S HERE!
SORRY, FOLKS. THIS ELEVATOR'S OUT OF ORDER.
ULTIMATE PLAN PHASE THREE.
NOVA? YOU TOO?
>SIGH< MAYBE PETER'S RIGHT. I HAVE TO LEARN WHEN ENOUGH IS ENOUGH.
WOULD A BIG, STRONG SUPER HERO LIKE TO ESCORT ME OUT OF THE BUILDING? I'LL LET YOU BUY ME LUNCH.
OH YEAH!

SO... ARE YOU A VIETNAMESE BARBECUE SANDWICH KIND OF GAL, OR--

I'M THE KIND OF GAL...

..WHO KNOWS HOW TO GET PAST A NOOB LIKE YOU!

DINC!

HEY! NOT COOL!

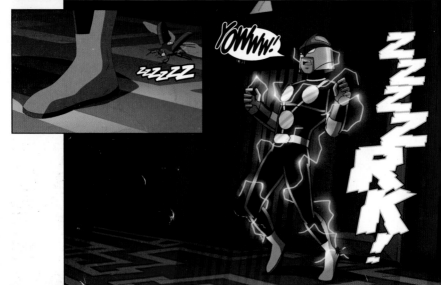

YOWWW!

ZZZZZ

ZZZZ RK!

HERE WE GO! SOON I'LL BE FACE-TO-FACE WITH J. JONAH JAMESON HIMS--

WHAT'S HAPPENING?

CRSHH!

SOMETHING'S WRONG WITH THE ELEVATOR.

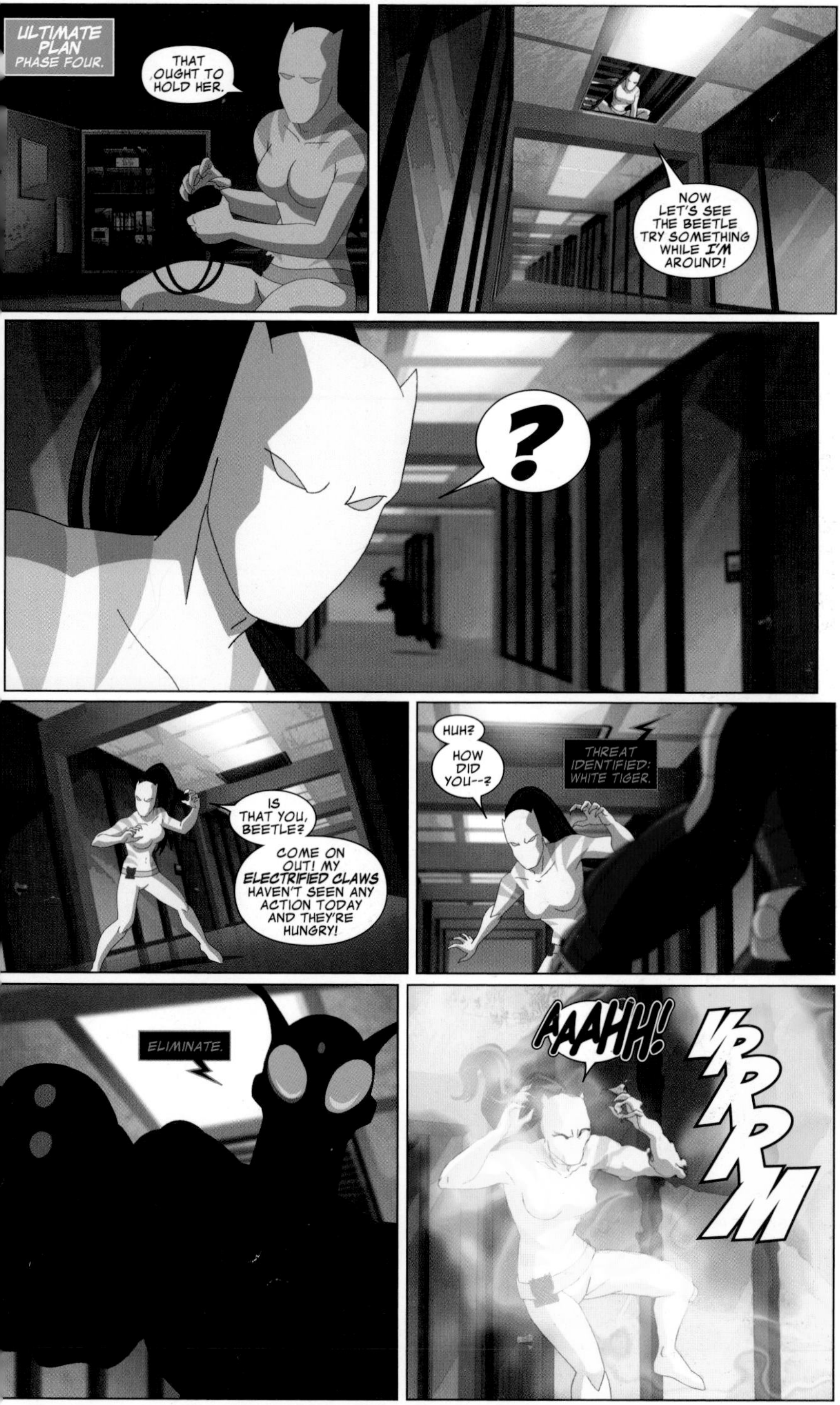
ULTIMATE PLAN PHASE FOUR.
THAT OUGHT TO HOLD HER.
NOW LET'S SEE THE BEETLE TRY SOMETHING WHILE I'M AROUND!
?
IS THAT YOU, BEETLE?
COME ON OUT! MY ELECTRIFIED CLAWS HAVEN'T SEEN ANY ACTION TODAY AND THEY'RE HUNGRY!
HUH?
HOW DID YOU--?
THREAT IDENTIFIED: WHITE TIGER.
ELIMINATE.
AAAHH!
VRRRM

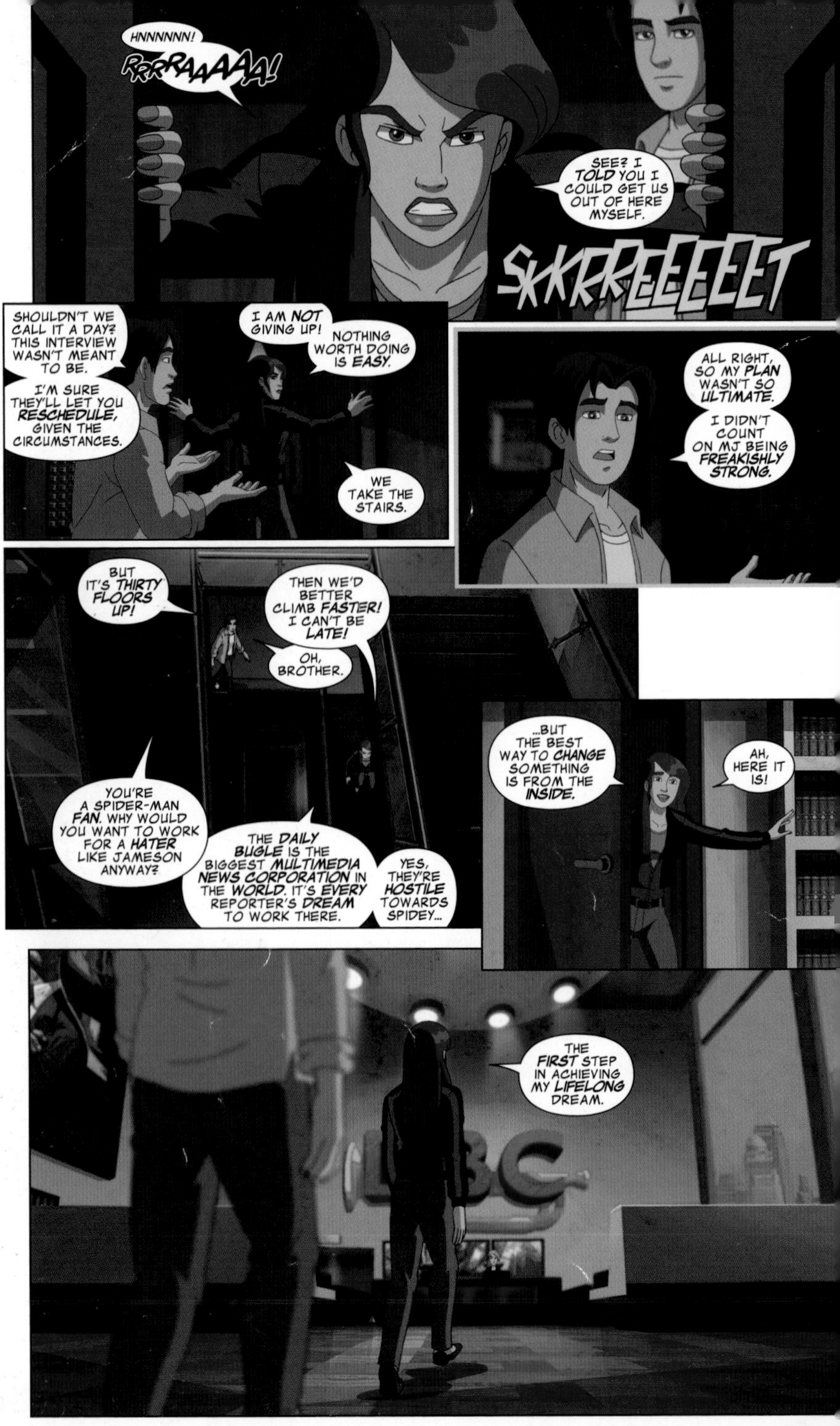

HNNNNNN!
RRRRAAAAAA!
SEE? I TOLD YOU I COULD GET US OUT OF HERE MYSELF.
SKKRREEEEET
SHOULDN'T WE CALL IT A DAY? THIS INTERVIEW WASN'T MEANT TO BE.
I'M SURE THEY'LL LET YOU RESCHEDULE, GIVEN THE CIRCUMSTANCES.
I AM NOT GIVING UP!
NOTHING WORTH DOING IS EASY.
WE TAKE THE STAIRS.
ALL RIGHT, SO MY PLAN WASN'T SO ULTIMATE.
I DIDN'T COUNT ON MJ BEING FREAKISHLY STRONG.
BUT IT'S THIRTY FLOORS UP!
THEN WE'D BETTER CLIMB FASTER! I CAN'T BE LATE!
OH, BROTHER.
YOU'RE A SPIDER-MAN FAN. WHY WOULD YOU WANT TO WORK FOR A HATER LIKE JAMESON ANYWAY?
THE DAILY BUGLE IS THE BIGGEST MULTIMEDIA NEWS CORPORATION IN THE WORLD. IT'S EVERY REPORTER'S DREAM TO WORK THERE.
YES, THEY'RE HOSTILE TOWARDS SPIDEY...
...BUT THE BEST WAY TO CHANGE SOMETHING IS FROM THE INSIDE.
AH, HERE IT IS!
THE FIRST STEP IN ACHIEVING MY LIFELONG DREAM.

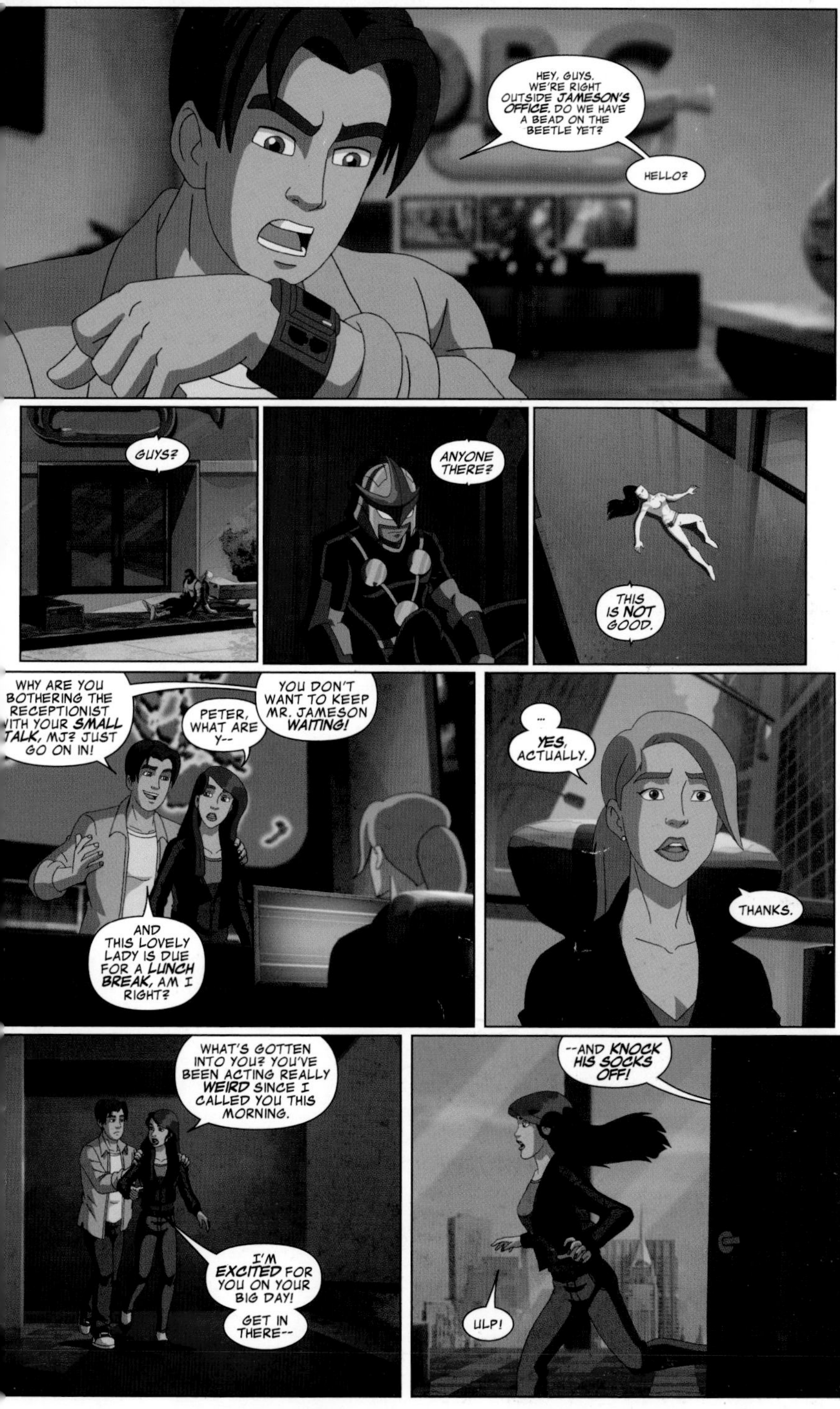

HEY, GUYS. WE'RE RIGHT OUTSIDE JAMESON'S OFFICE. DO WE HAVE A BEAD ON THE BEETLE YET?
HELLO?
GUYS?
ANYONE THERE?
THIS IS NOT GOOD.
WHY ARE YOU BOTHERING THE RECEPTIONIST WITH YOUR SMALL TALK, MJ? JUST GO ON IN!
PETER, WHAT ARE Y--
YOU DON'T WANT TO KEEP MR. JAMESON WAITING!
AND THIS LOVELY LADY IS DUE FOR A LUNCH BREAK, AM I RIGHT?
...
YES, ACTUALLY.
THANKS.
WHAT'S GOTTEN INTO YOU? YOU'VE BEEN ACTING REALLY WEIRD SINCE I CALLED YOU THIS MORNING.
I'M EXCITED FOR YOU ON YOUR BIG DAY!
GET IN THERE--
--AND KNOCK HIS SOCKS OFF!
ULP!

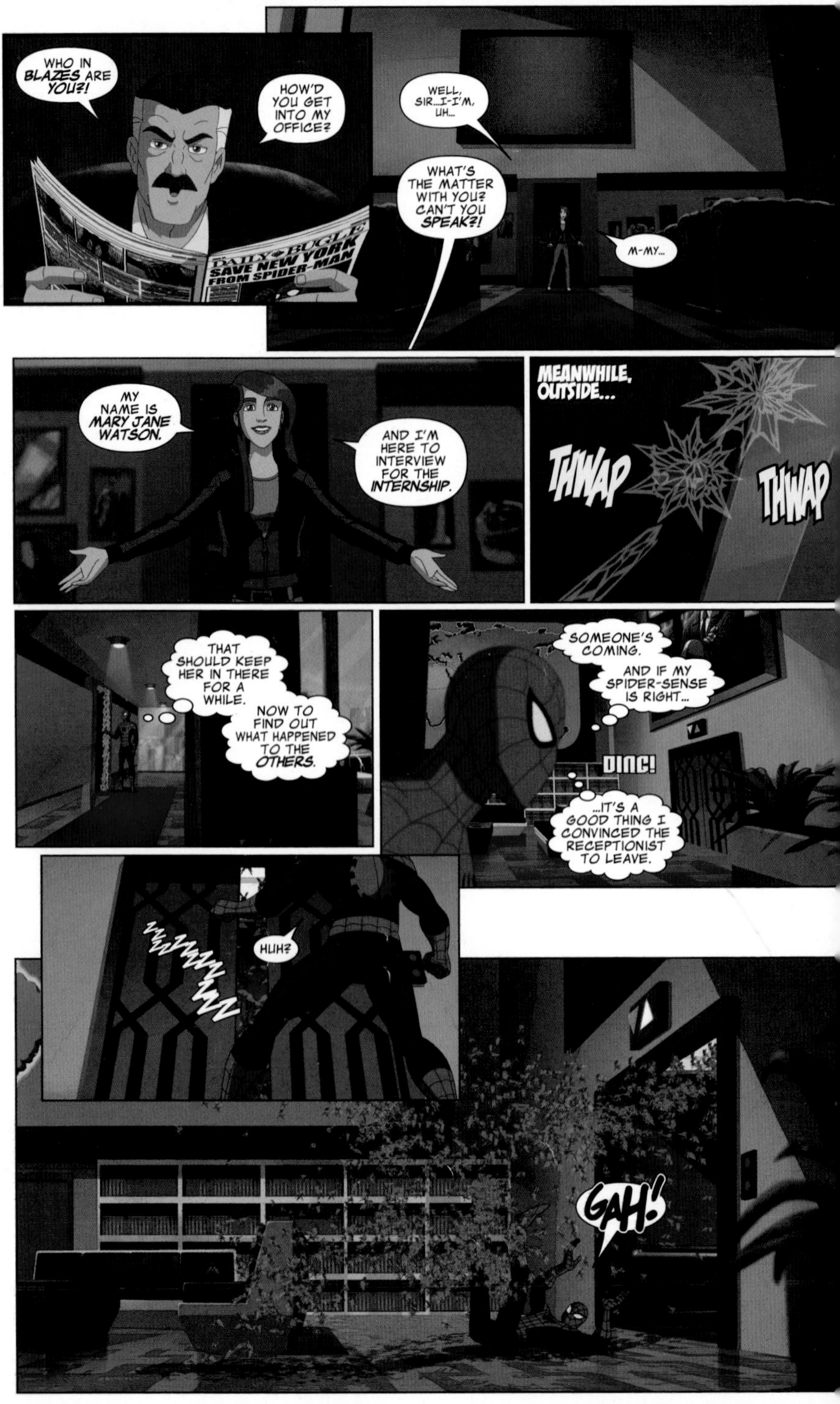
WHO IN BLAZES ARE YOU?!
HOW'D YOU GET INTO MY OFFICE?
DAILY BUGLE
SAVE NEW YORK FROM SPIDER-MAN
WELL, SIR...I-I'M, UH...
WHAT'S THE MATTER WITH YOU? CAN'T YOU SPEAK?!
M-MY...
MY NAME IS MARY JANE WATSON.
AND I'M HERE TO INTERVIEW FOR THE INTERNSHIP.
MEANWHILE, OUTSIDE...
THWAP
THWAP
THAT SHOULD KEEP HER IN THERE FOR A WHILE.
NOW TO FIND OUT WHAT HAPPENED TO THE OTHERS.
SOMEONE'S COMING.
AND IF MY SPIDER-SENSE IS RIGHT...
DING!
...IT'S A GOOD THING I CONVINCED THE RECEPTIONIST TO LEAVE.
HUH?
GAH!

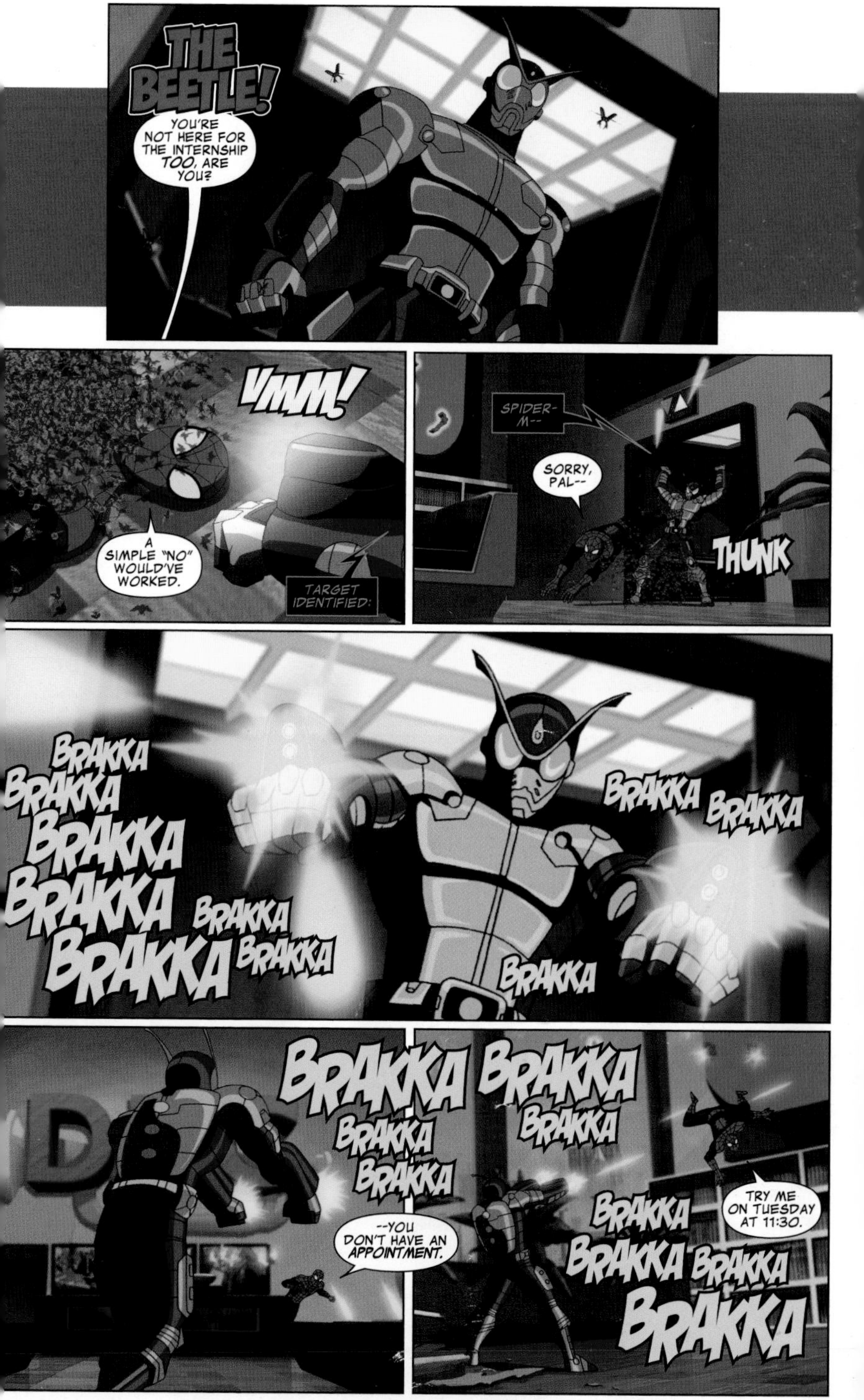
THE BEETLE!
YOU'RE NOT HERE FOR THE INTERNSHIP TOO, ARE YOU?
VMM!
A SIMPLE "NO" WOULD'VE WORKED.
TARGET IDENTIFIED:
SPIDER-M--
SORRY, PAL--
THUNK
BRAKKA BRAKKA BRAKKA BRAKKA BRAKKA BRAKKA BRAKKA
BRAKKA BRAKKA
BRAKKA
BRAKKA BRAKKA
BRAKKA BRAKKA
BRAKKA BRAKKA
--YOU DON'T HAVE AN APPOINTMENT.
TRY ME ON TUESDAY AT 11:30.
BRAKKA BRAKKA BRAKKA BRAKKA

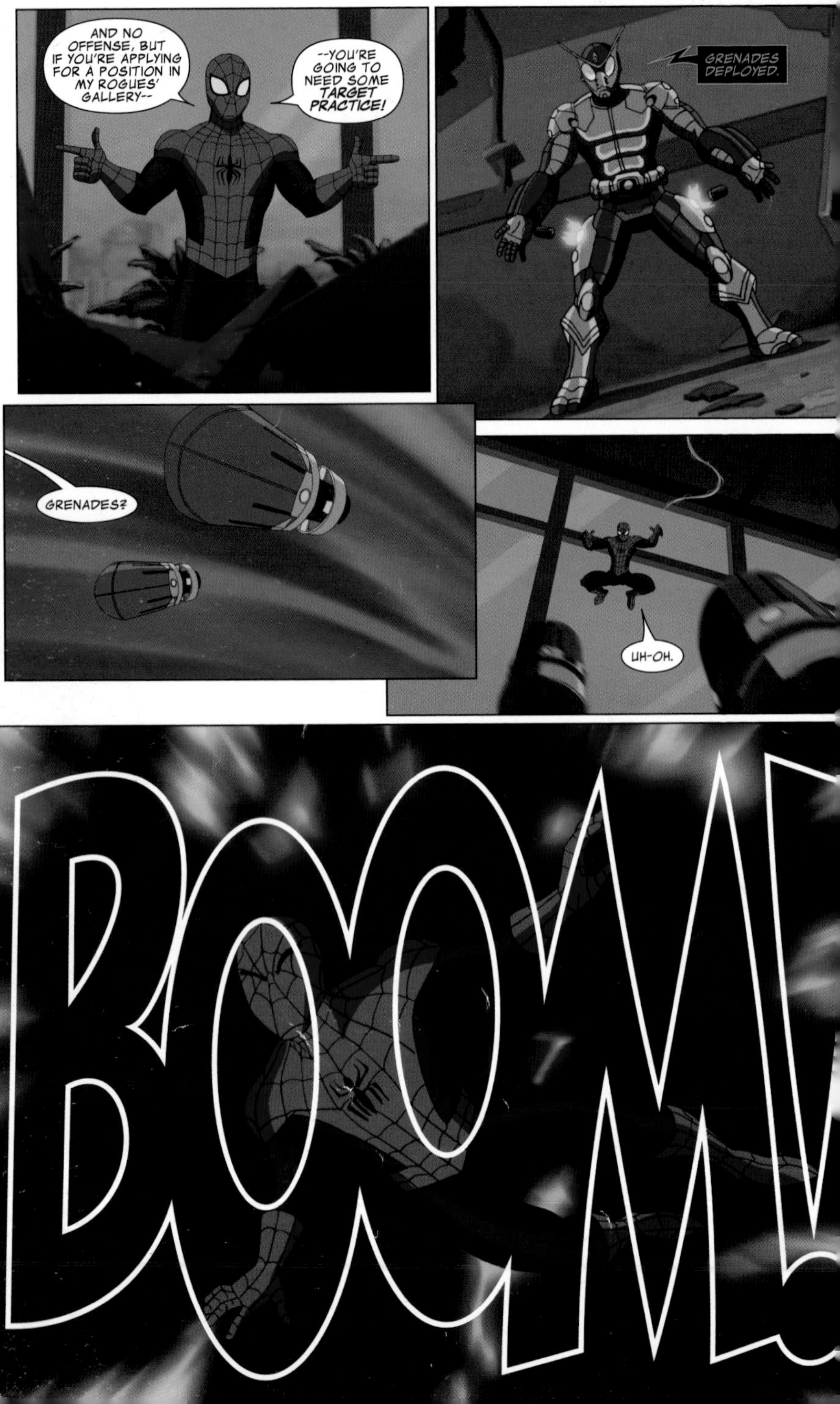
AND NO OFFENSE, BUT IF YOU'RE APPLYING FOR A POSITION IN MY ROGUES' GALLERY--
--YOU'RE GOING TO NEED SOME TARGET PRACTICE!
GRENADES DEPLOYED.
GRENADES?
UH-OH.
BOOM!

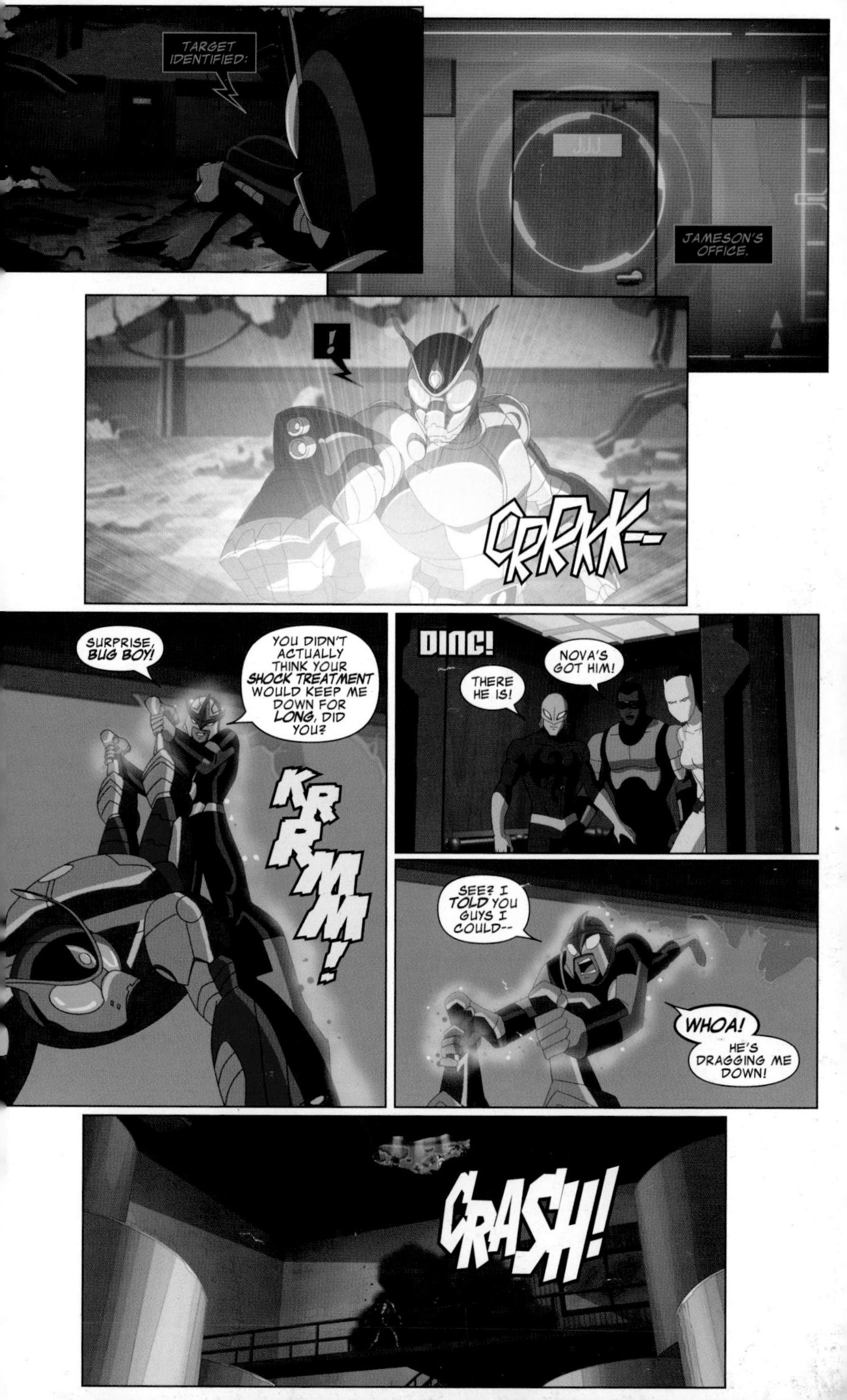

TARGET IDENTIFIED:
JAMESON'S OFFICE.
!
CRRKK--
SURPRISE, BUG BOY!
YOU DIDN'T ACTUALLY THINK YOUR SHOCK TREATMENT WOULD KEEP ME DOWN FOR LONG, DID YOU?
KRRMM!
DING!
THERE HE IS!
NOVA'S GOT HIM!
SEE? I TOLD YOU GUYS I COULD--
WHOA! HE'S DRAGGING ME DOWN!
CRASH!

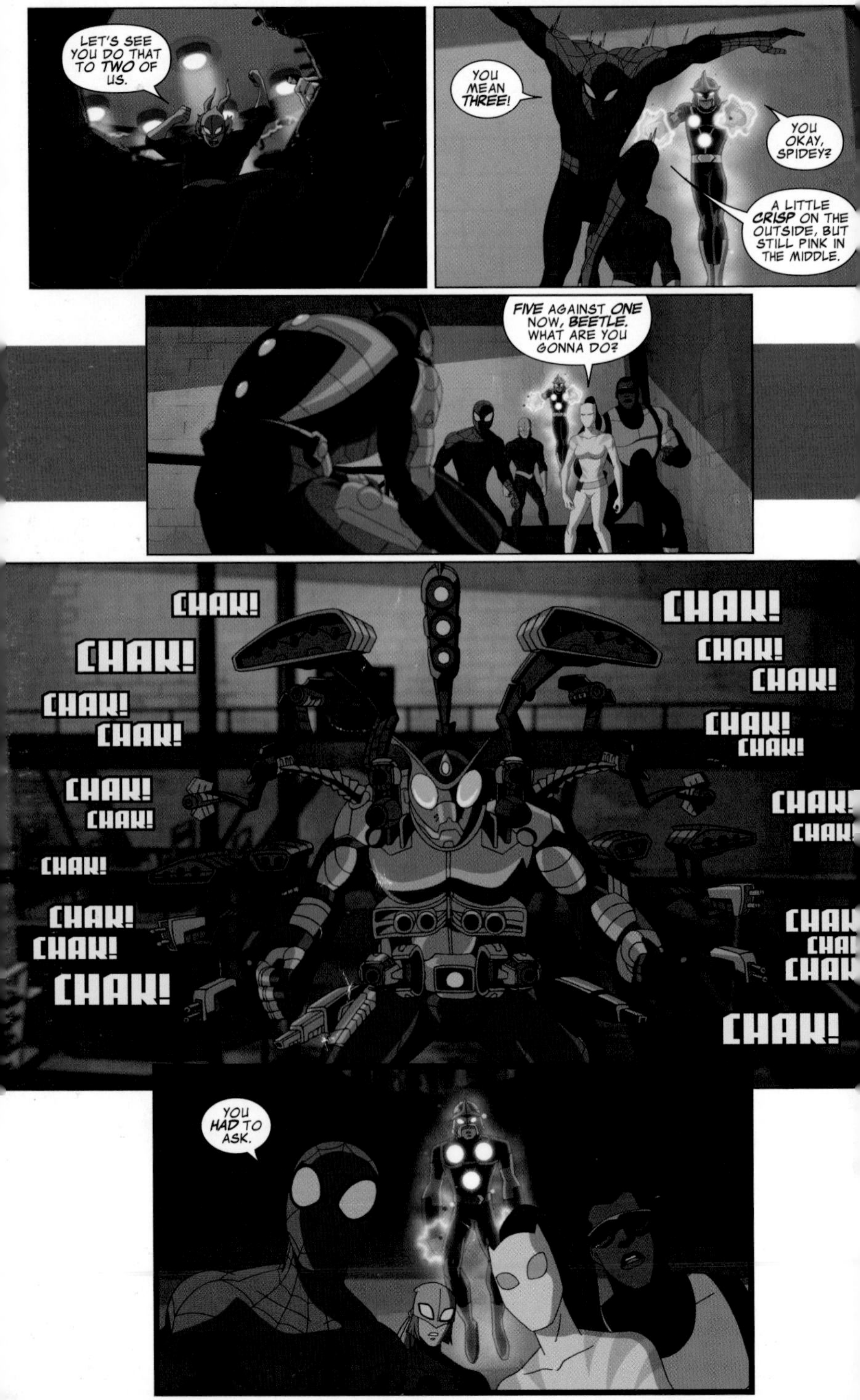

LET'S SEE YOU DO THAT TO TWO OF US.
YOU MEAN THREE!
YOU OKAY, SPIDEY?
A LITTLE CRISP ON THE OUTSIDE, BUT STILL PINK IN THE MIDDLE.
FIVE AGAINST ONE NOW, BEETLE. WHAT ARE YOU GONNA DO?
CHAK!
CHAK!
CHAK!
CHAK!
CHAK!
CHAK!
CHAK!
CHAK!
CHAK!
CHAK!
CHAK!
CHAK!
CHAK!
CHAK!
CHAK!
CHAK!
CHAK!
YOU HAD TO ASK.

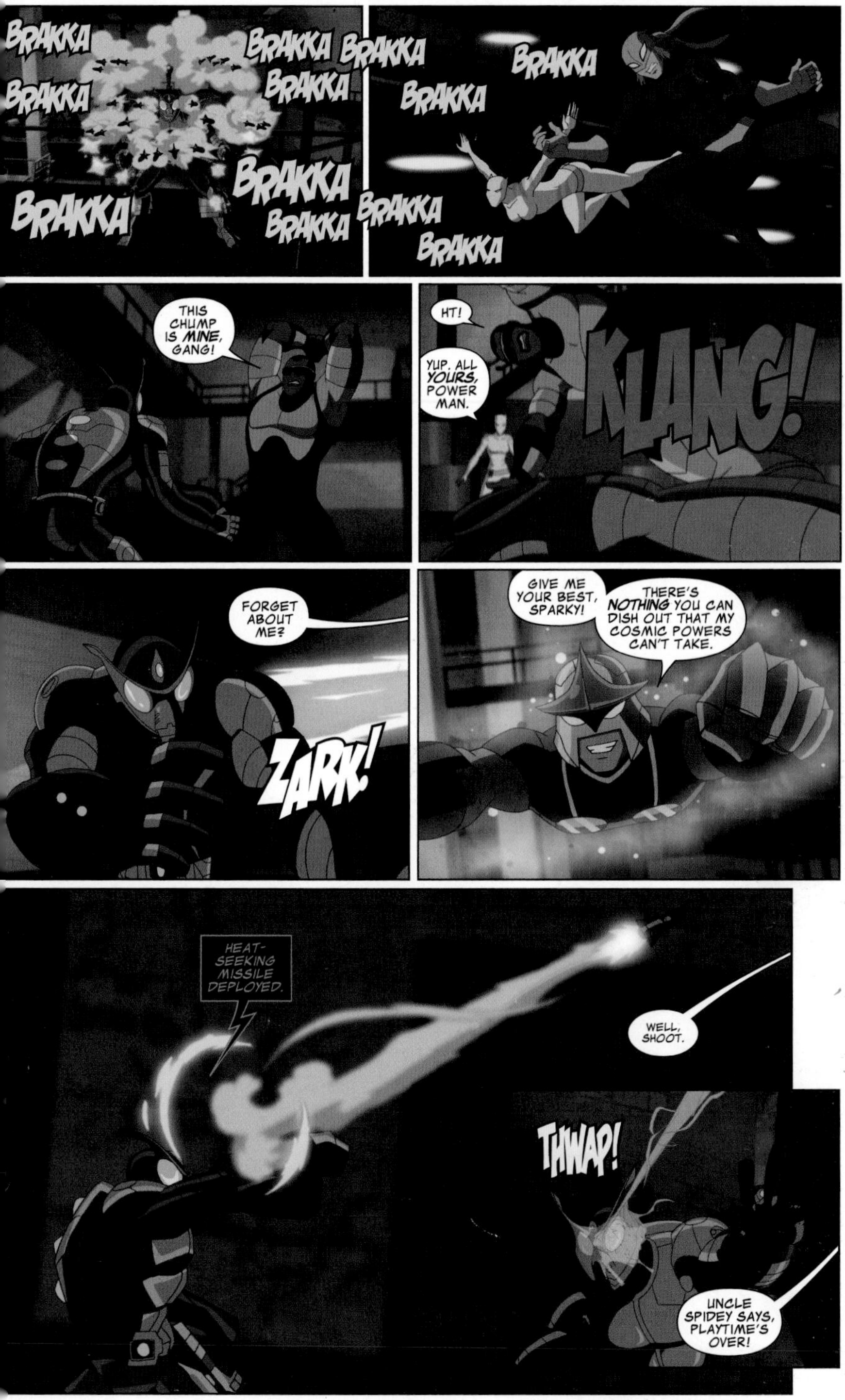
BRAKKA
BRAKKA
BRAKKA
BRAKKA
BRAKKA
BRAKKA
BRAKKA
BRAKKA
BRAKKA
BRAKKA
BRAKKA
BRAKKA
THIS CHUMP IS MINE, GANG!
HT!
YUP. ALL YOURS, POWER MAN.
KLANG!
FORGET ABOUT ME?
ZARK!
GIVE ME YOUR BEST, SPARKY!
THERE'S NOTHING YOU CAN DISH OUT THAT MY COSMIC POWERS CAN'T TAKE.
HEAT-SEEKING MISSILE DEPLOYED.
WELL, SHOOT.
THWAP!
UNCLE SPIDEY SAYS, PLAYTIME'S OVER!

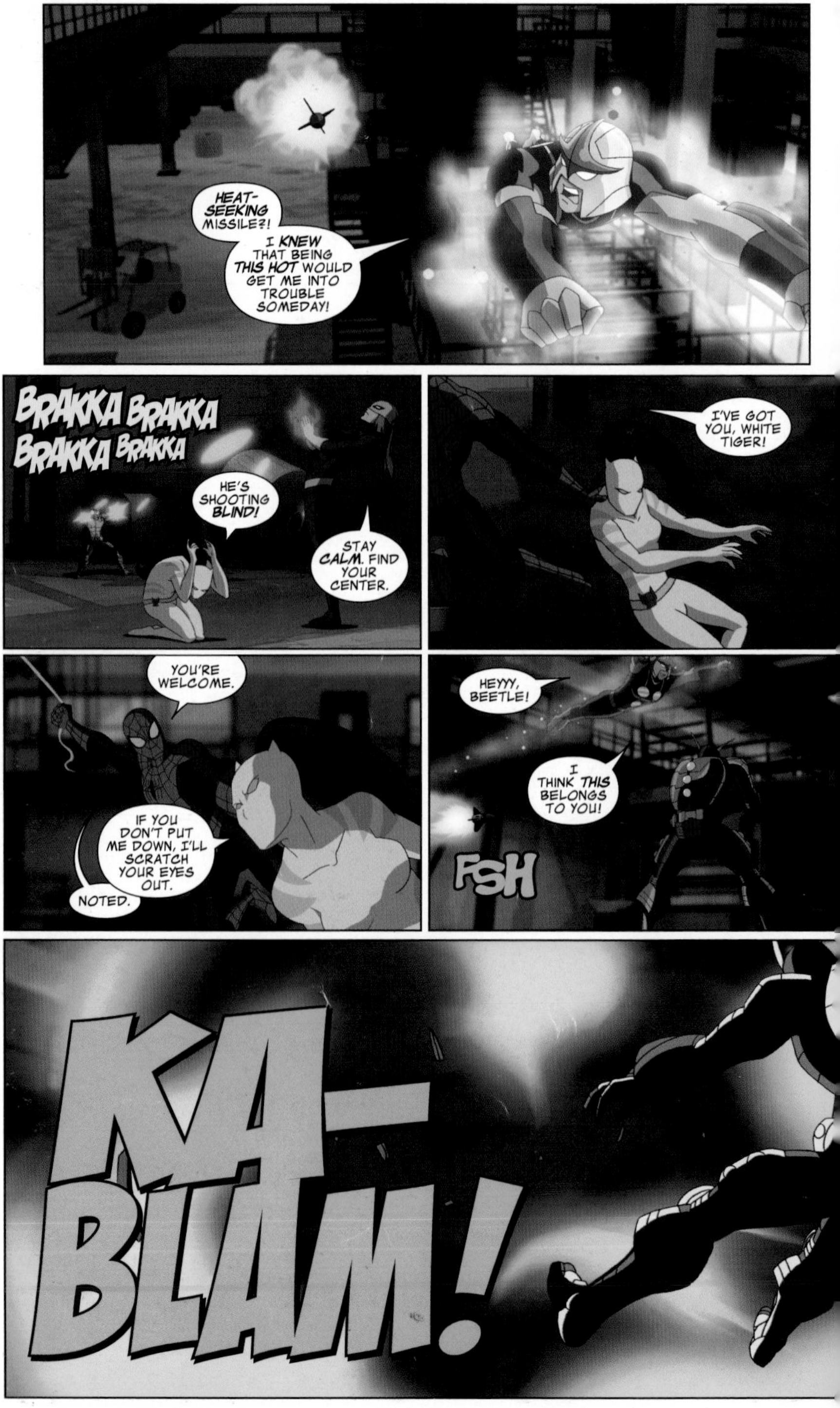

HEAT-SEEKING MISSILE?! I KNEW THAT BEING THIS HOT WOULD GET ME INTO TROUBLE SOMEDAY!
BRAKKA BRAKKA BRAKKA BRAKKA
HE'S SHOOTING BLIND!
STAY CALM. FIND YOUR CENTER.
I'VE GOT YOU, WHITE TIGER!
YOU'RE WELCOME.
IF YOU DON'T PUT ME DOWN, I'LL SCRATCH YOUR EYES OUT.
NOTED.
HEYYY, BEETLE!
I THINK THIS BELONGS TO YOU!
FSH
KA-BLAM!

POWER MAN--**THIS** LOOKS LIKE IT COULD HOLD HIM.

YOU'RE THE ONLY ONE HERE **STRONG** ENOUGH TO PULL IT OFF.

IT'S WORTH A SHOT.

YO! WANT TO PLAY A **GAME?** IT'S CALLED--

--RING AROUND THE BEETLE!

DANGEROUS ENERGY COMPRESSION-- ZZZZZZK--

CLUDD!

MISSION ACCOMPLISHED, TEAM!

NOT BAD FOR A FIRST **OFFICIAL** OUTING IF I DO SAY SO MY--

KKKRRRRKKK

KRABBLE

HRNN!

LOCATING TARGET. JAMESON.

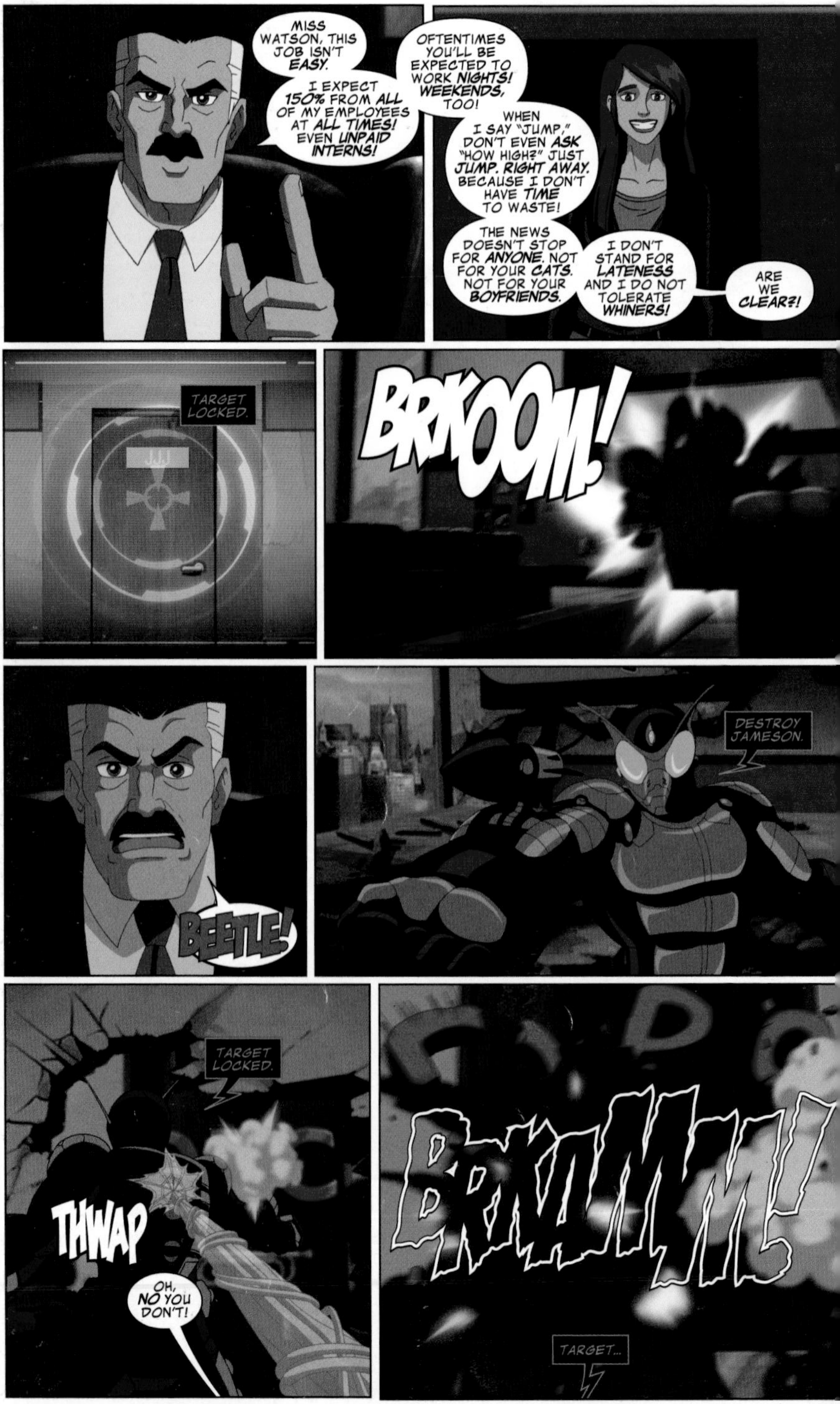

MISS WATSON, THIS JOB ISN'T EASY.
I EXPECT 150% FROM ALL OF MY EMPLOYEES AT ALL TIMES! EVEN UNPAID INTERNS!
OFTENTIMES YOU'LL BE EXPECTED TO WORK NIGHTS! WEEKENDS, TOO!
WHEN I SAY "JUMP," DON'T EVEN ASK "HOW HIGH?" JUST JUMP. RIGHT AWAY. BECAUSE I DON'T HAVE TIME TO WASTE!
THE NEWS DOESN'T STOP FOR ANYONE. NOT FOR YOUR CATS. NOT FOR YOUR BOYFRIENDS.
I DON'T STAND FOR LATENESS AND I DO NOT TOLERATE WHINERS!
ARE WE CLEAR?!
TARGET LOCKED.
JJJ
BRKOOM!
BEETLE!
DESTROY JAMESON.
TARGET LOCKED.
THWAP
OH, NO YOU DON'T!
BRKOOMM!
TARGET...

...MISSED?

YES, YOU DID.

BUT *I* WON'T.

KRAM!

ZzZzRRKK--

WHAT ARE YOU ALL DOING IN MY OFFICE?!

A VIDEO PROJECTION?

ALL THIS TIME--ALL YOUR *BRAVADO* ABOUT NOT NEEDING TO BE PROTECTED--

AND HE WASN'T EVEN IN THE BUILDING.

I SHOULD'VE *KNOWN* YOU WERE INVOLVED SOMEHOW, WEB-HEAD!

THERE'S NO WAY OUT OF THIS NOW, I'VE CAUGHT YOU TRESPASSING RED-HANDED!

I'VE ALWAYS SAID YOU WERE A MENACE TO THIS CITY, AND I FINALLY HAVE THE PROOF IVEZZ BEENZZRK *WAZZJITINGZZ FORZZ?!*

HOW ABOUT THAT?

SOMEONE PULLED THE PLUG.

THERE GOES HIS PROOF.

THANKS FOR SAVING MY LIFE *AGAIN*, SPIDER-MAN.

AW, SHUCKS. IT WAS NOTHING.

COME ON, ROMEO. WE'RE TAKING BEETLE TO S.H.I.E.L.D.

SORRY, WHITE TIGER WAITS FOR NO ONE!

SAY HI TO YOUR FRIEND *PETER* FOR ME!

PETER?

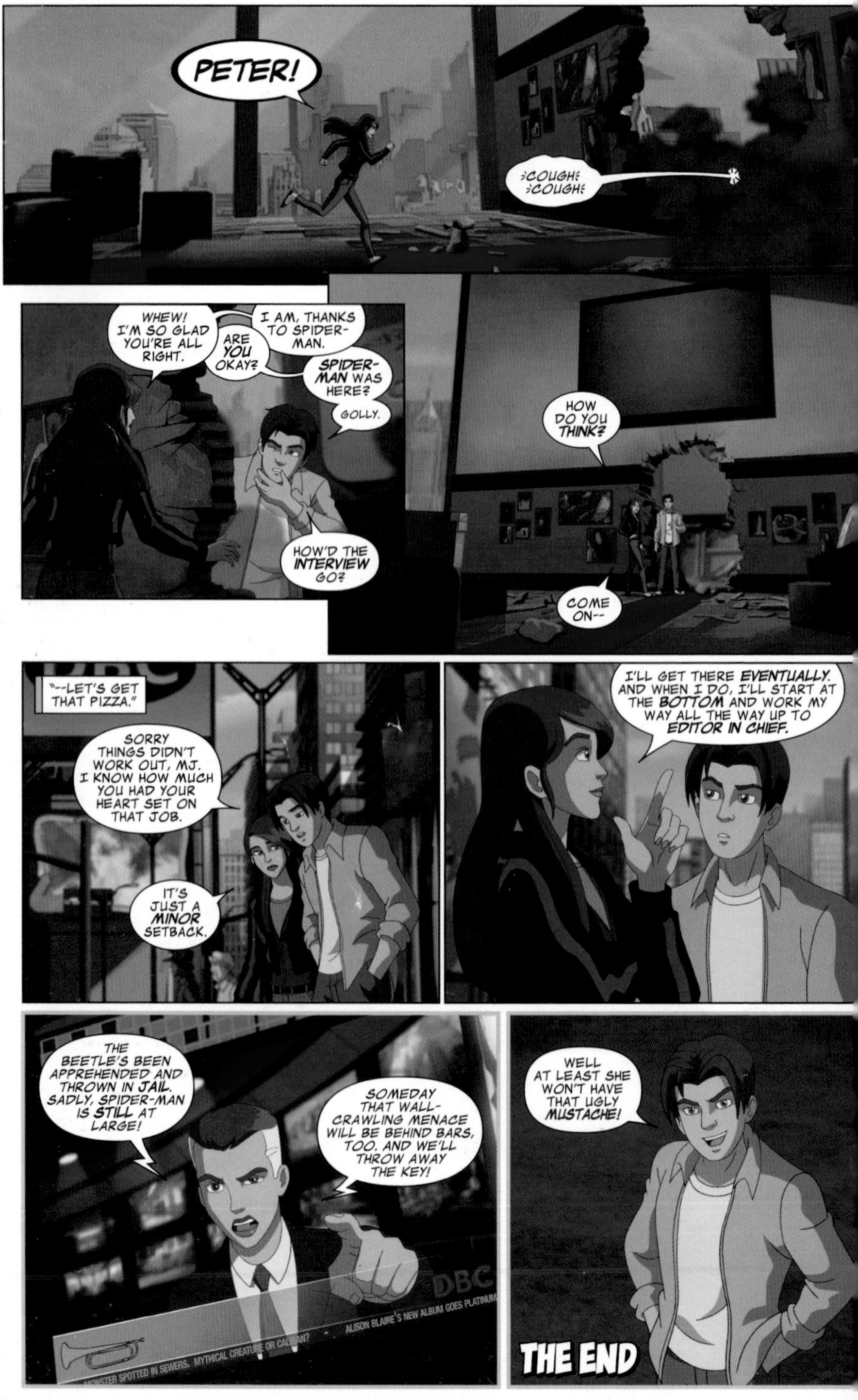

PETER!
COUGH *COUGH*
WHEW! I'M SO GLAD YOU'RE ALL RIGHT.
ARE YOU OKAY?
I AM, THANKS TO SPIDER-MAN.
SPIDER-MAN WAS HERE?
GOLLY.
HOW'D THE INTERVIEW GO?
HOW DO YOU THINK?
COME ON--
"--LET'S GET THAT PIZZA."
SORRY THINGS DIDN'T WORK OUT, MJ. I KNOW HOW MUCH YOU HAD YOUR HEART SET ON THAT JOB.
IT'S JUST A MINOR SETBACK.
I'LL GET THERE EVENTUALLY. AND WHEN I DO, I'LL START AT THE BOTTOM AND WORK MY WAY ALL THE WAY UP TO EDITOR IN CHIEF.
THE BEETLE'S BEEN APPREHENDED AND THROWN IN JAIL. SADLY, SPIDER-MAN IS STILL AT LARGE!
SOMEDAY THAT WALL-CRAWLING MENACE WILL BE BEHIND BARS, TOO. AND WE'LL THROW AWAY THE KEY!
DBC
ALISON BLAIRE'S NEW ALBUM GOES PLATINUM
WELL AT LEAST SHE WON'T HAVE THAT UGLY MUSTACHE!
THE END

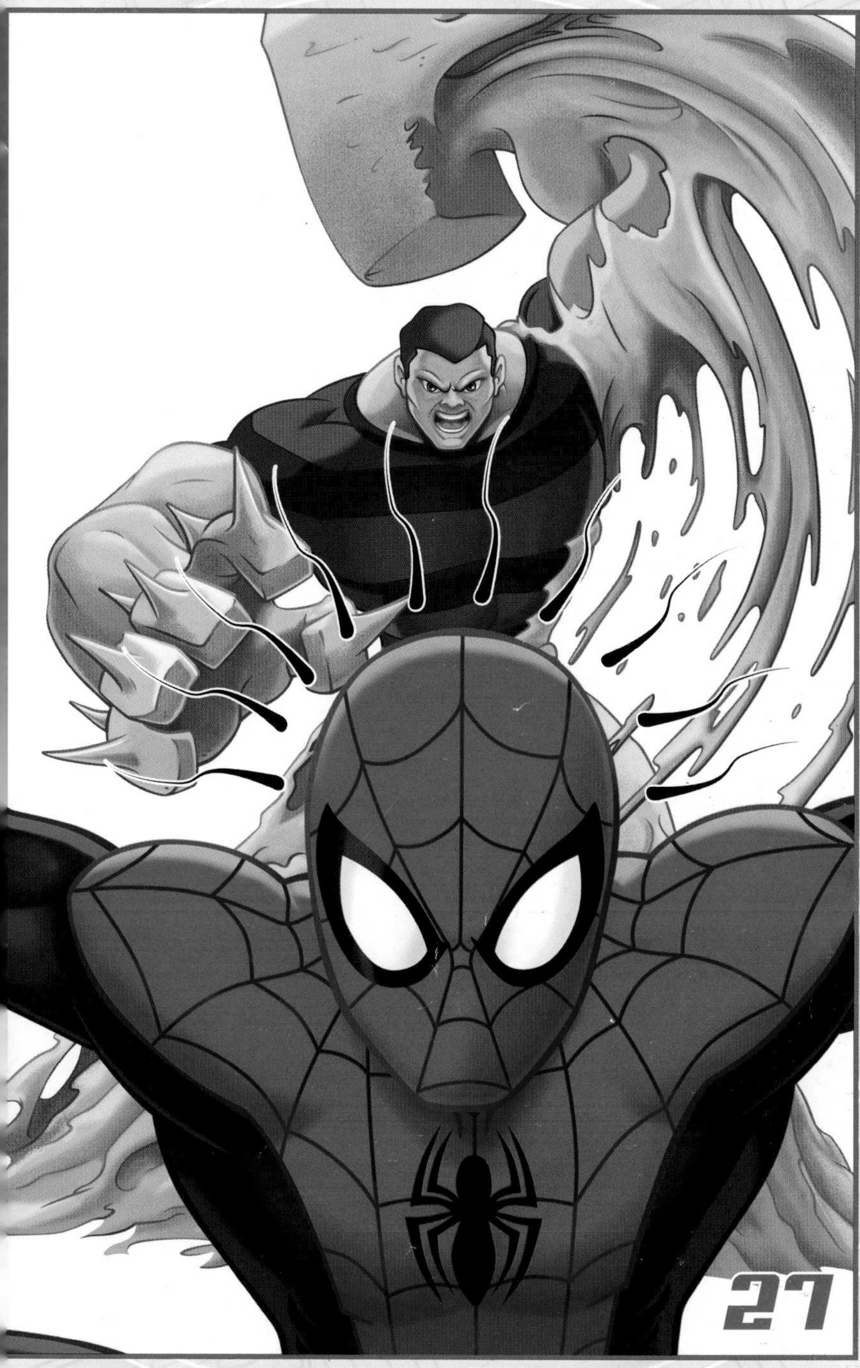
27

Based on "Snow Day"

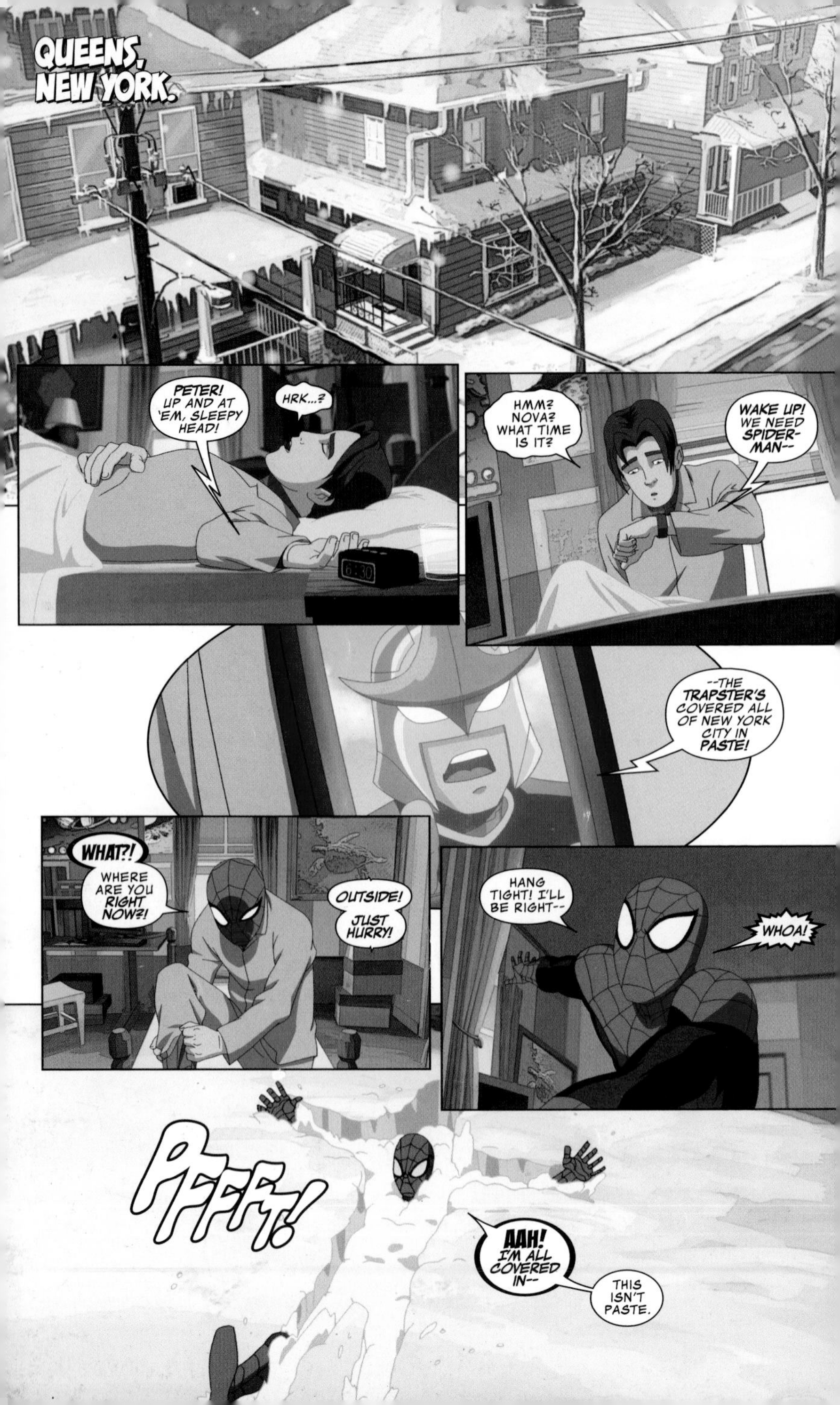
QUEENS, NEW YORK.
PETER! UP AND AT 'EM, SLEEPY HEAD!
HRK...?
HMM? NOVA? WHAT TIME IS IT?
WAKE UP! WE NEED SPIDER-MAN--
--THE TRAPSTER'S COVERED ALL OF NEW YORK CITY IN PASTE!
WHAT?! WHERE ARE YOU RIGHT NOW?!
OUTSIDE! JUST HURRY!
HANG TIGHT! I'LL BE RIGHT--
WHOA!
PFFFT!
AAH! I'M ALL COVERED IN--
THIS ISN'T PASTE.

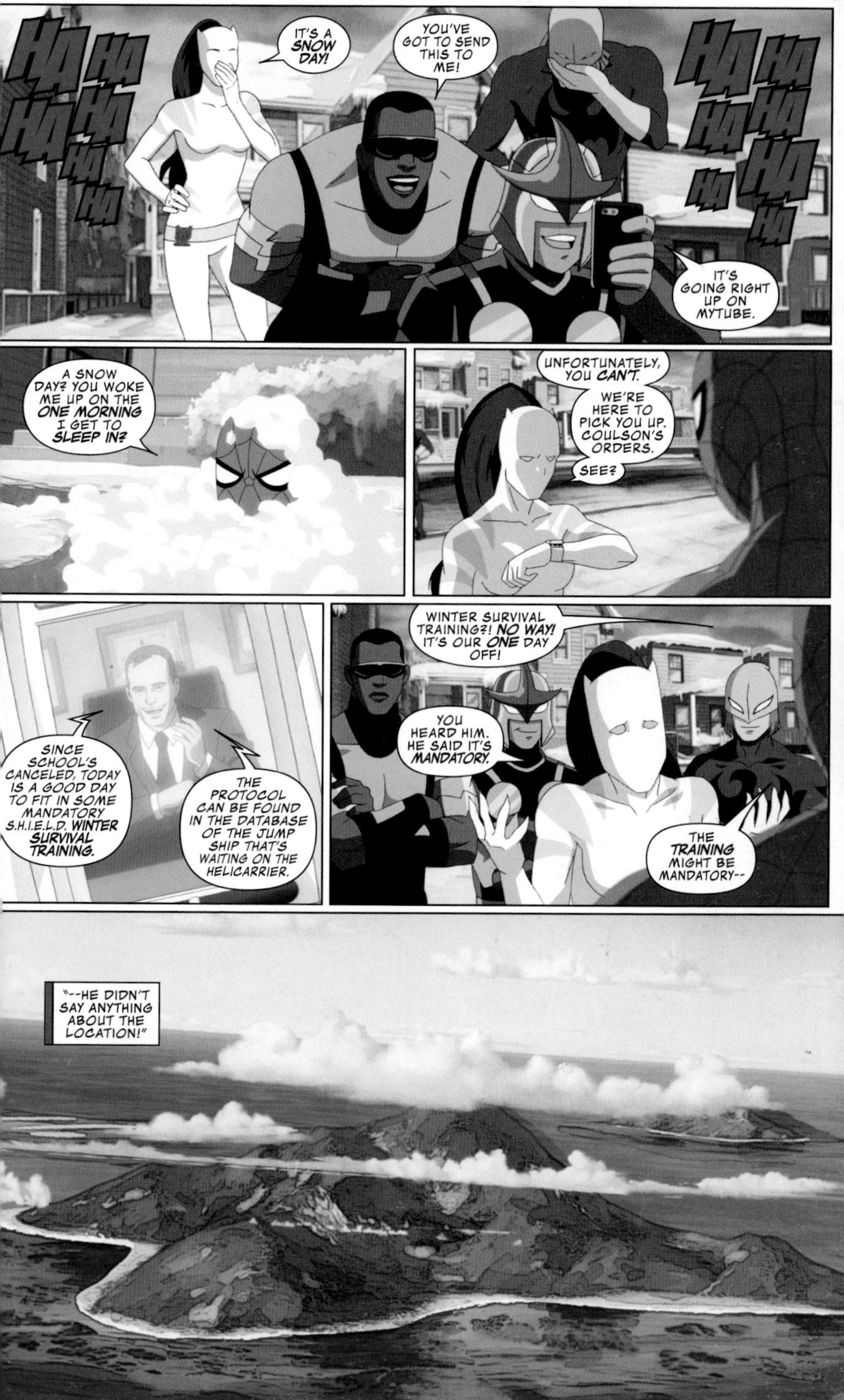
HA HA HA HA HA HA HA
IT'S A SNOW DAY!
YOU'VE GOT TO SEND THIS TO ME!
HA HA HA HA HA HA HA HA
IT'S GOING RIGHT UP ON MYTUBE.
A SNOW DAY? YOU WOKE ME UP ON THE ONE MORNING I GET TO SLEEP IN?
UNFORTUNATELY, YOU CAN'T.
WE'RE HERE TO PICK YOU UP. COULSON'S ORDERS.
SEE?
SINCE SCHOOL'S CANCELED, TODAY IS A GOOD DAY TO FIT IN SOME MANDATORY S.H.I.E.L.D. WINTER SURVIVAL TRAINING.
THE PROTOCOL CAN BE FOUND IN THE DATABASE OF THE JUMP SHIP THAT'S WAITING ON THE HELICARRIER.
WINTER SURVIVAL TRAINING?! NO WAY! IT'S OUR ONE DAY OFF!
YOU HEARD HIM. HE SAID IT'S MANDATORY.
THE TRAINING MIGHT BE MANDATORY--
"--HE DIDN'T SAY ANYTHING ABOUT THE LOCATION!"

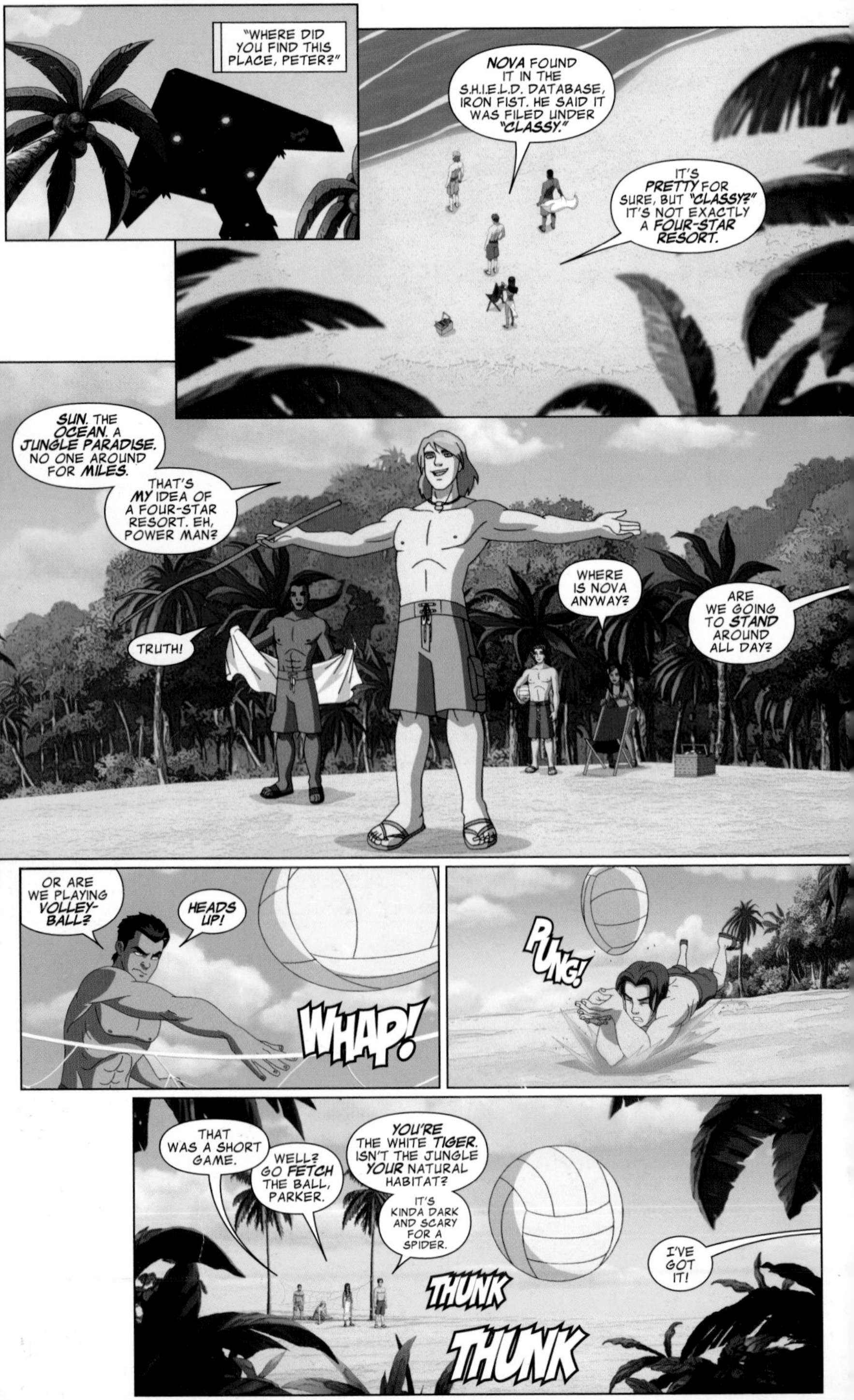
"WHERE DID YOU FIND THIS PLACE, PETER?"
NOVA FOUND IT IN THE S.H.I.E.L.D. DATABASE, IRON FIST. HE SAID IT WAS FILED UNDER "CLASSY."
IT'S PRETTY FOR SURE, BUT "CLASSY?" IT'S NOT EXACTLY A FOUR-STAR RESORT.
SUN. THE OCEAN. A JUNGLE PARADISE. NO ONE AROUND FOR MILES.
THAT'S MY IDEA OF A FOUR-STAR RESORT. EH, POWER MAN?
TRUTH!
WHERE IS NOVA ANYWAY?
ARE WE GOING TO STAND AROUND ALL DAY?
OR ARE WE PLAYING VOLLEY-BALL?
HEADS UP!
WHAP!
PUNG!
THAT WAS A SHORT GAME.
WELL? GO FETCH THE BALL, PARKER.
YOU'RE THE WHITE TIGER. ISN'T THE JUNGLE YOUR NATURAL HABITAT?
IT'S KINDA DARK AND SCARY FOR A SPIDER.
I'VE GOT IT!
THUNK
THUNK

MY NAME'S SANDY. I LIVE HERE. CAN I PLAY?

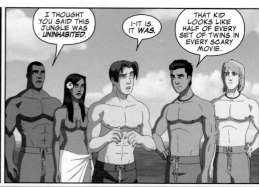

I THOUGHT YOU SAID THIS JUNGLE WAS UNINHABITED.

I-IT IS. IT WAS.

THAT KID LOOKS LIKE HALF OF EVERY SET OF TWINS IN EVERY SCARY MOVIE.

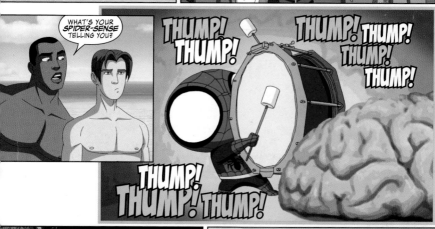

WHAT'S YOUR SPIDER-SENSE TELLING YOU?

THUMP! THUMP!

THUMP! THUMP! THUMP! THUMP!

THUMP! THUMP! THUMP!

SERIOUSLY? HE'S JUST A KID.

AND HE'S OUT HERE ALL ALONE.

CATCH ME IF YOU CAN!

ARE WE SUITING UP?

SO MUCH FOR OUR VACATION.

MOMENTS LATER...

YO, KID! WHERE ARE YOU?

SANDY! COME OUT, COME OUT WHEREVER YOU ARE!

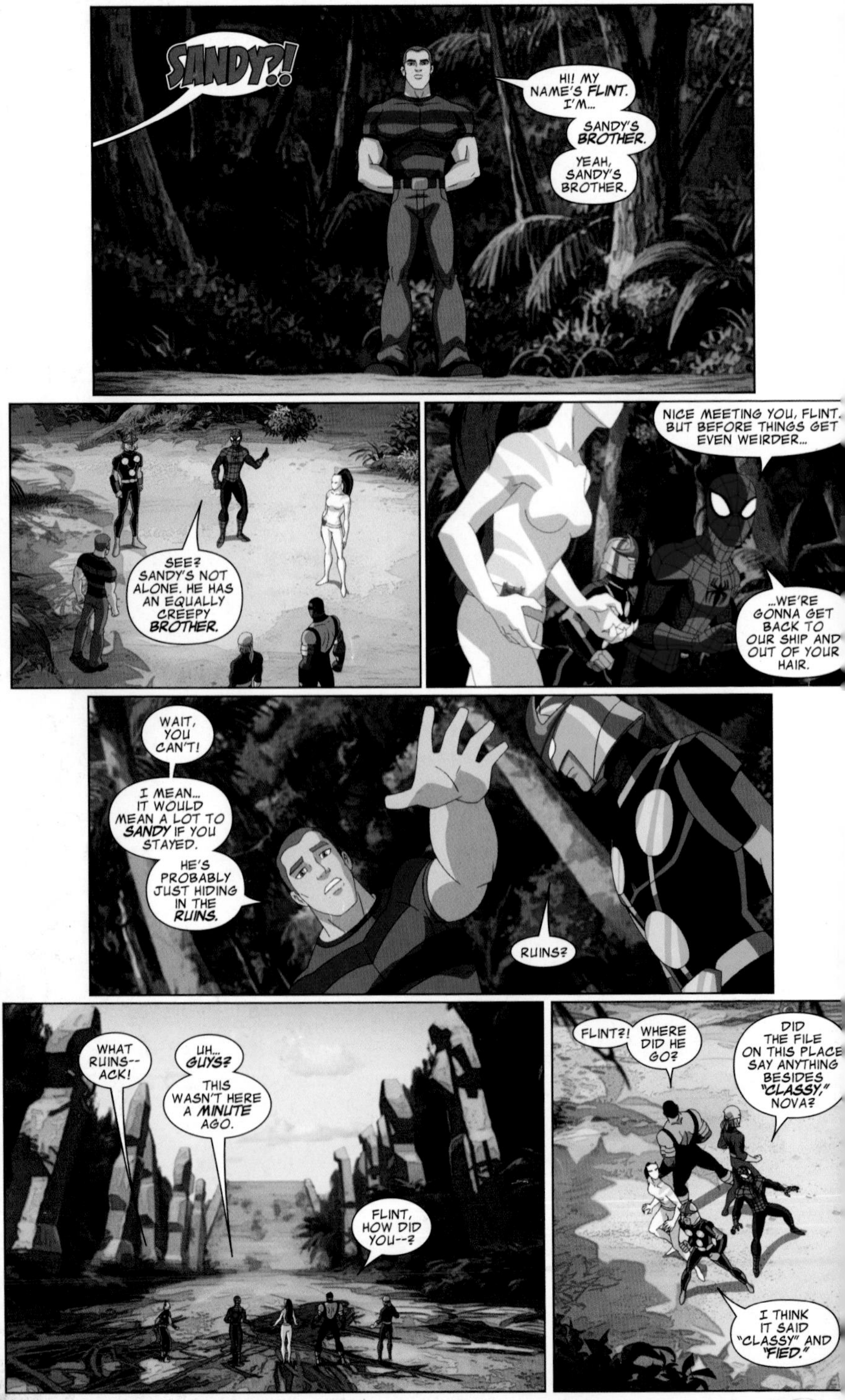
SANDY?!
HI! MY NAME'S FLINT. I'M...
SANDY'S BROTHER.
YEAH, SANDY'S BROTHER.
SEE? SANDY'S NOT ALONE. HE HAS AN EQUALLY CREEPY BROTHER.
NICE MEETING YOU, FLINT. BUT BEFORE THINGS GET EVEN WEIRDER...
...WE'RE GONNA GET BACK TO OUR SHIP AND OUT OF YOUR HAIR.
WAIT, YOU CAN'T!
I MEAN... IT WOULD MEAN A LOT TO SANDY IF YOU STAYED.
HE'S PROBABLY JUST HIDING IN THE RUINS.
RUINS?
WHAT RUINS-- ACK!
UH... GUYS?
THIS WASN'T HERE A MINUTE AGO.
FLINT, HOW DID YOU--?
FLINT?!
WHERE DID HE GO?
DID THE FILE ON THIS PLACE SAY ANYTHING BESIDES "CLASSY," NOVA?
I THINK IT SAID "CLASSY" AND "FIED."

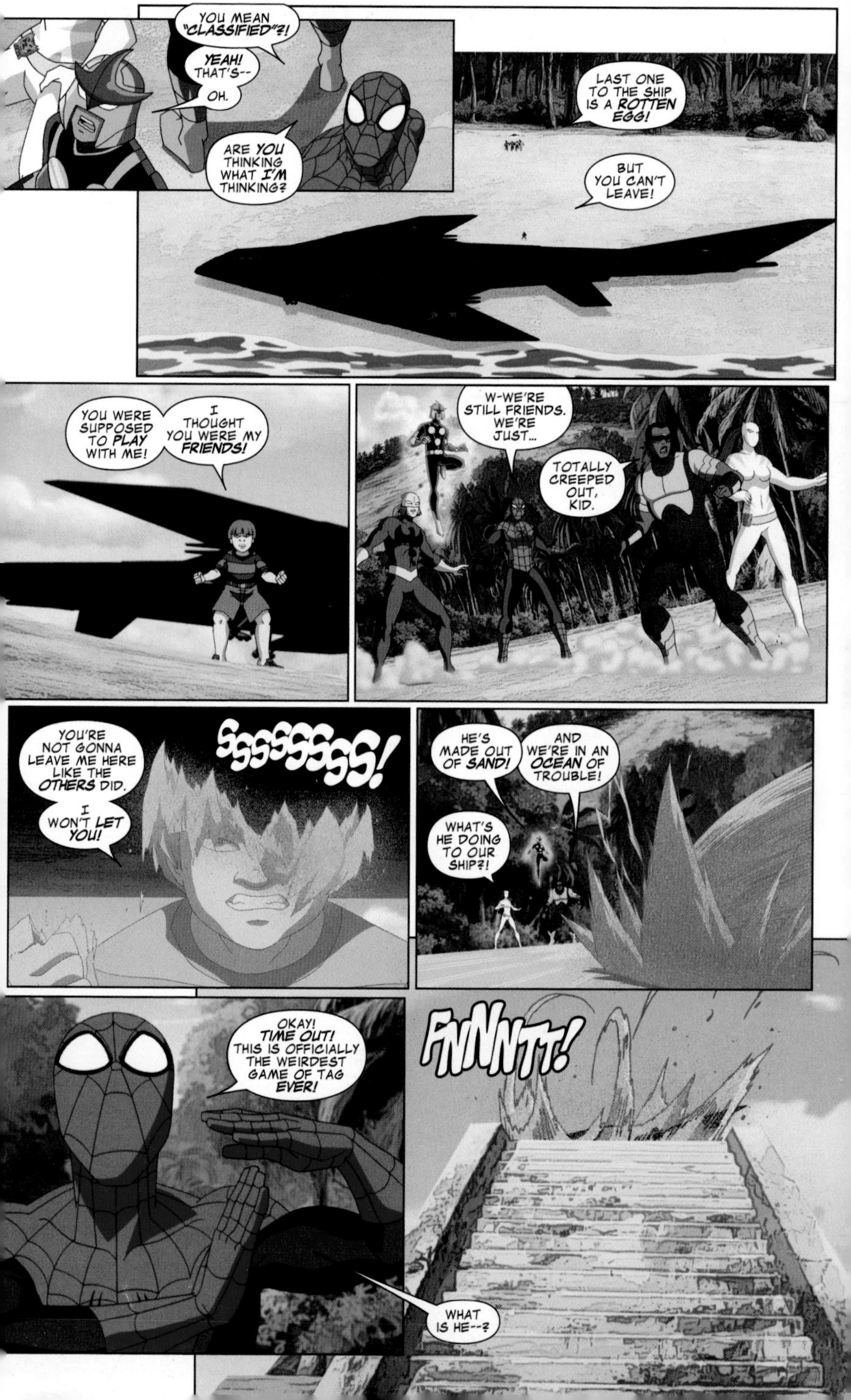
YOU MEAN "CLASSIFIED"?!
YEAH! THAT'S--
OH.
ARE YOU THINKING WHAT I'M THINKING?
LAST ONE TO THE SHIP IS A ROTTEN EGG!
BUT YOU CAN'T LEAVE!
YOU WERE SUPPOSED TO PLAY WITH ME!
I THOUGHT YOU WERE MY FRIENDS!
W-WE'RE STILL FRIENDS. WE'RE JUST...
TOTALLY CREEPED OUT, KID.
YOU'RE NOT GONNA LEAVE ME HERE LIKE THE OTHERS DID.
I WON'T LET YOU!
SSSSSSSS!
HE'S MADE OUT OF SAND!
AND WE'RE IN AN OCEAN OF TROUBLE!
WHAT'S HE DOING TO OUR SHIP?!
OKAY! TIME OUT! THIS IS OFFICIALLY THE WEIRDEST GAME OF TAG EVER!
WHAT IS HE--?
FNNNTT!

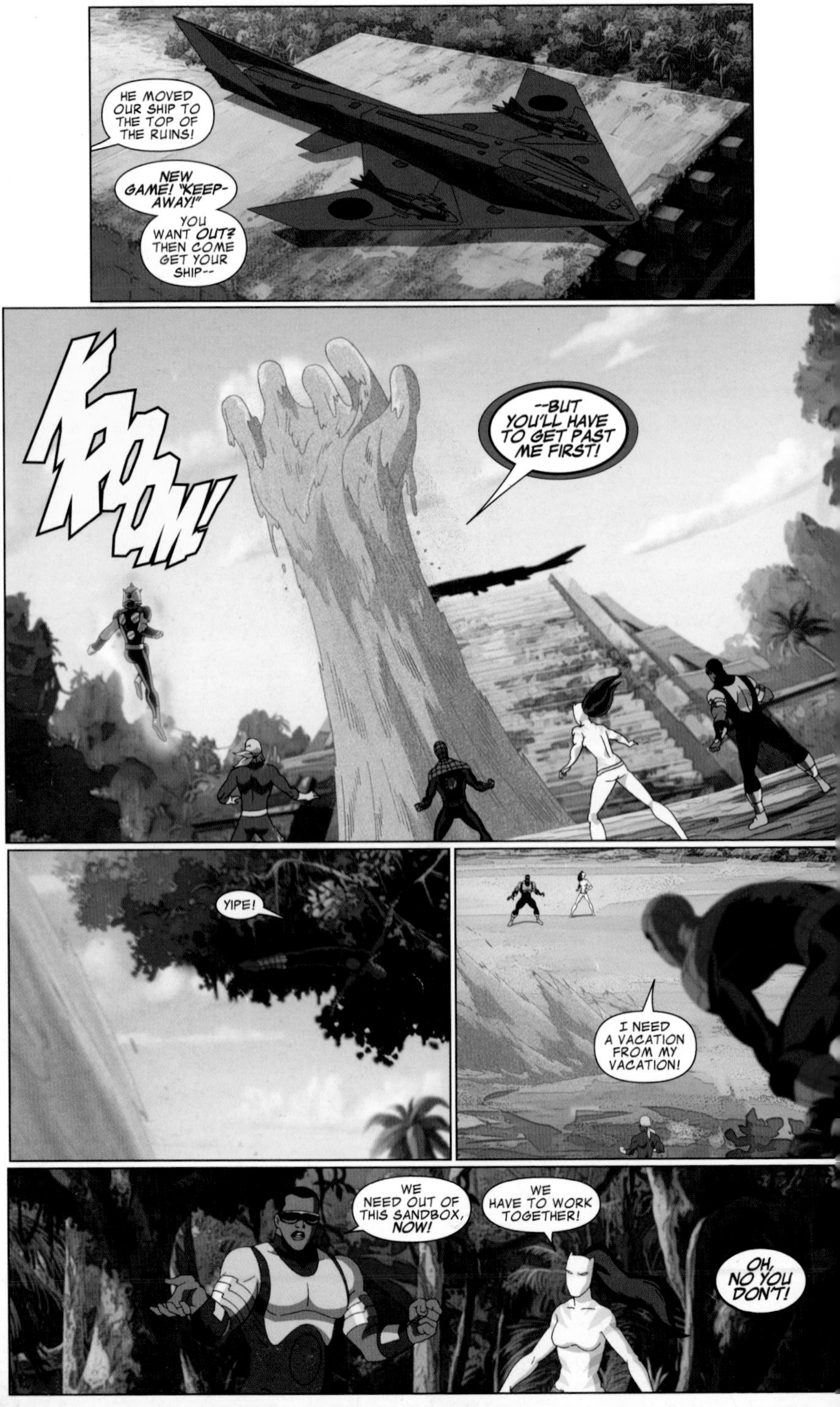
HE MOVED OUR SHIP TO THE TOP OF THE RUINS!
NEW GAME! "KEEP-AWAY!"
YOU WANT OUT? THEN COME GET YOUR SHIP--
KROOOM!
--BUT YOU'LL HAVE TO GET PAST ME FIRST!
YIPE!
I NEED A VACATION FROM MY VACATION!
WE NEED OUT OF THIS SANDBOX, NOW!
WE HAVE TO WORK TOGETHER!
OH, NO YOU DON'T!

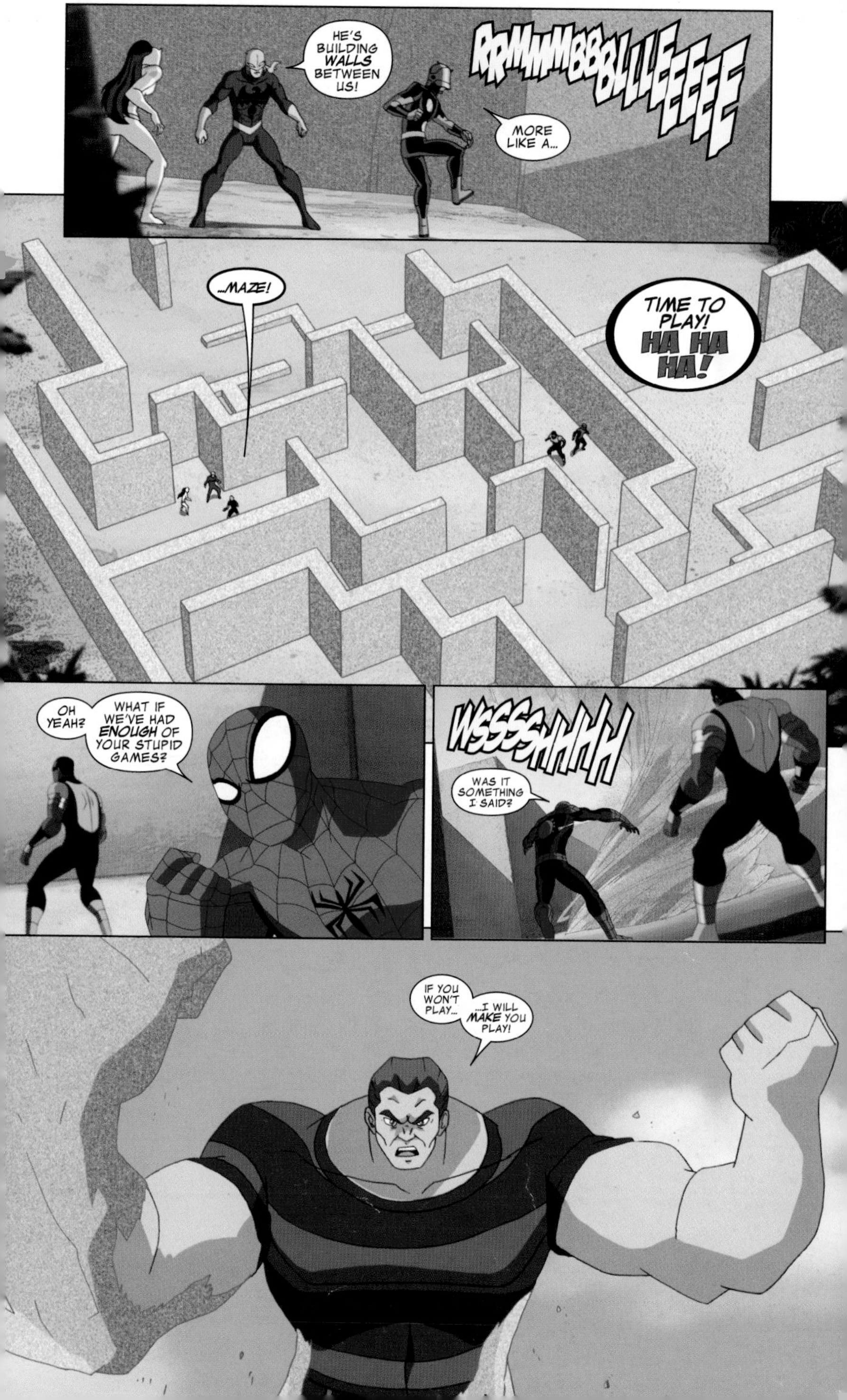
HE'S BUILDING WALLS BETWEEN US!
RRMMMBBBLLLEEEEE
MORE LIKE A...
...MAZE!
TIME TO PLAY! HA HA HA!
OH YEAH?
WHAT IF WE'VE HAD ENOUGH OF YOUR STUPID GAMES?
WSSSSHHHH
WAS IT SOMETHING I SAID?
IF YOU WON'T PLAY...
...I WILL MAKE YOU PLAY!

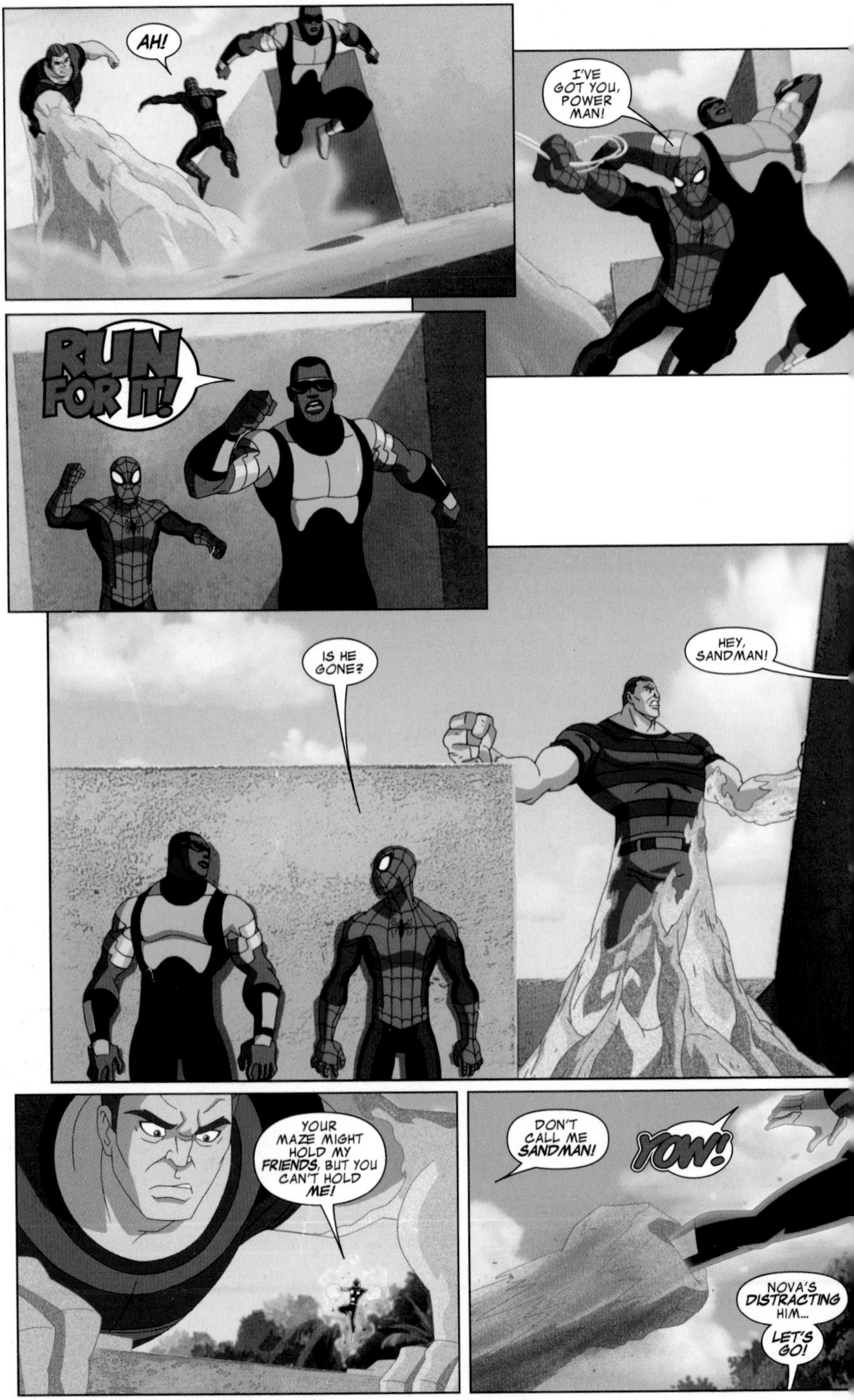

AH!
I'VE GOT YOU, POWER MAN!
RUN FOR IT!
IS HE GONE?
HEY, SANDMAN!
YOUR MAZE MIGHT HOLD MY FRIENDS, BUT YOU CAN'T HOLD ME!
DON'T CALL ME SANDMAN!
YOW!
NOVA'S DISTRACTING HIM...
LET'S GO!

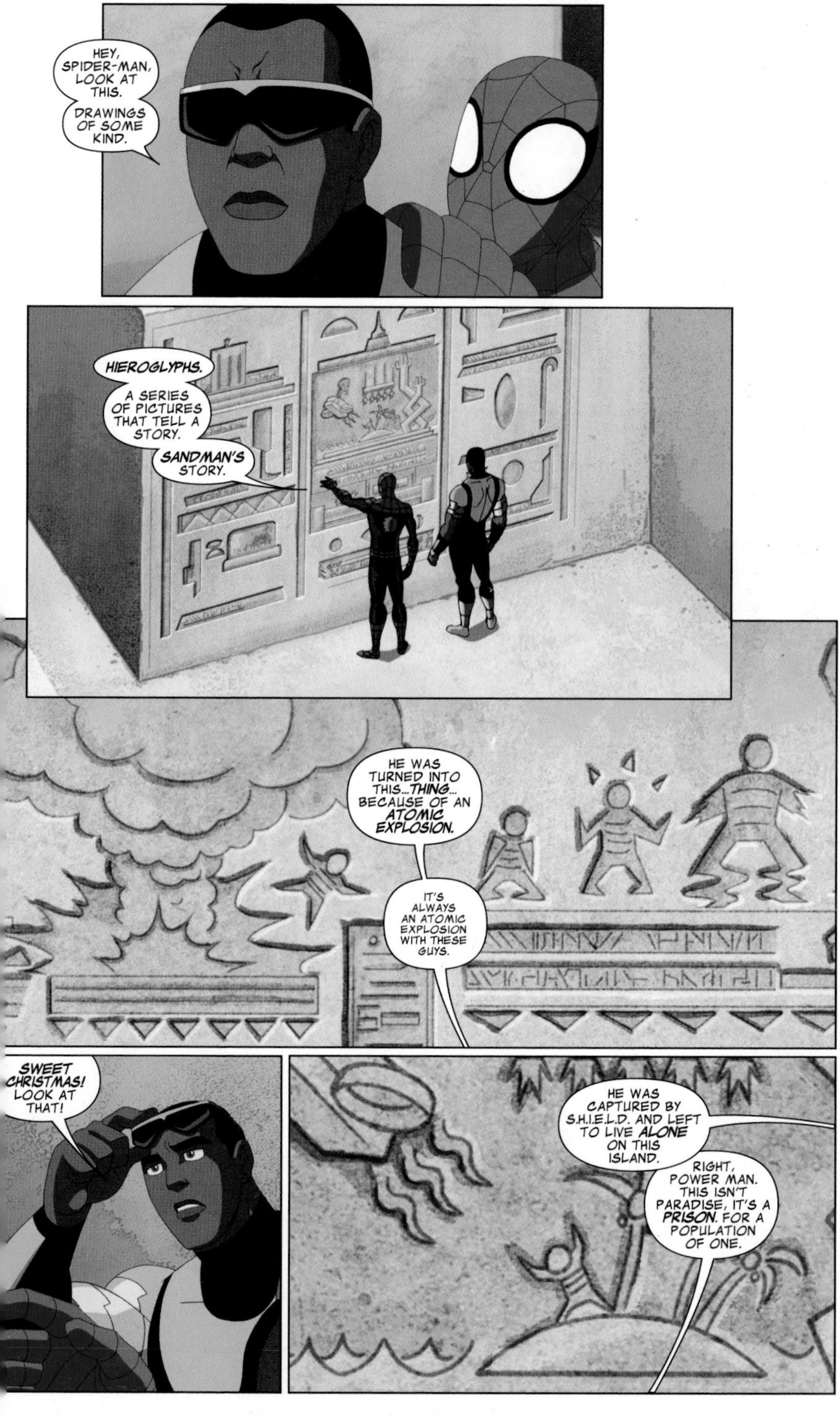
HEY, SPIDER-MAN, LOOK AT THIS.
DRAWINGS OF SOME KIND.
HIEROGLYPHS.
A SERIES OF PICTURES THAT TELL A STORY.
SANDMAN'S STORY.
HE WAS TURNED INTO THIS...THING... BECAUSE OF AN ATOMIC EXPLOSION.
IT'S ALWAYS AN ATOMIC EXPLOSION WITH THESE GUYS.
SWEET CHRISTMAS! LOOK AT THAT!
HE WAS CAPTURED BY S.H.I.E.L.D. AND LEFT TO LIVE ALONE ON THIS ISLAND.
RIGHT, POWER MAN. THIS ISN'T PARADISE, IT'S A PRISON. FOR A POPULATION OF ONE.

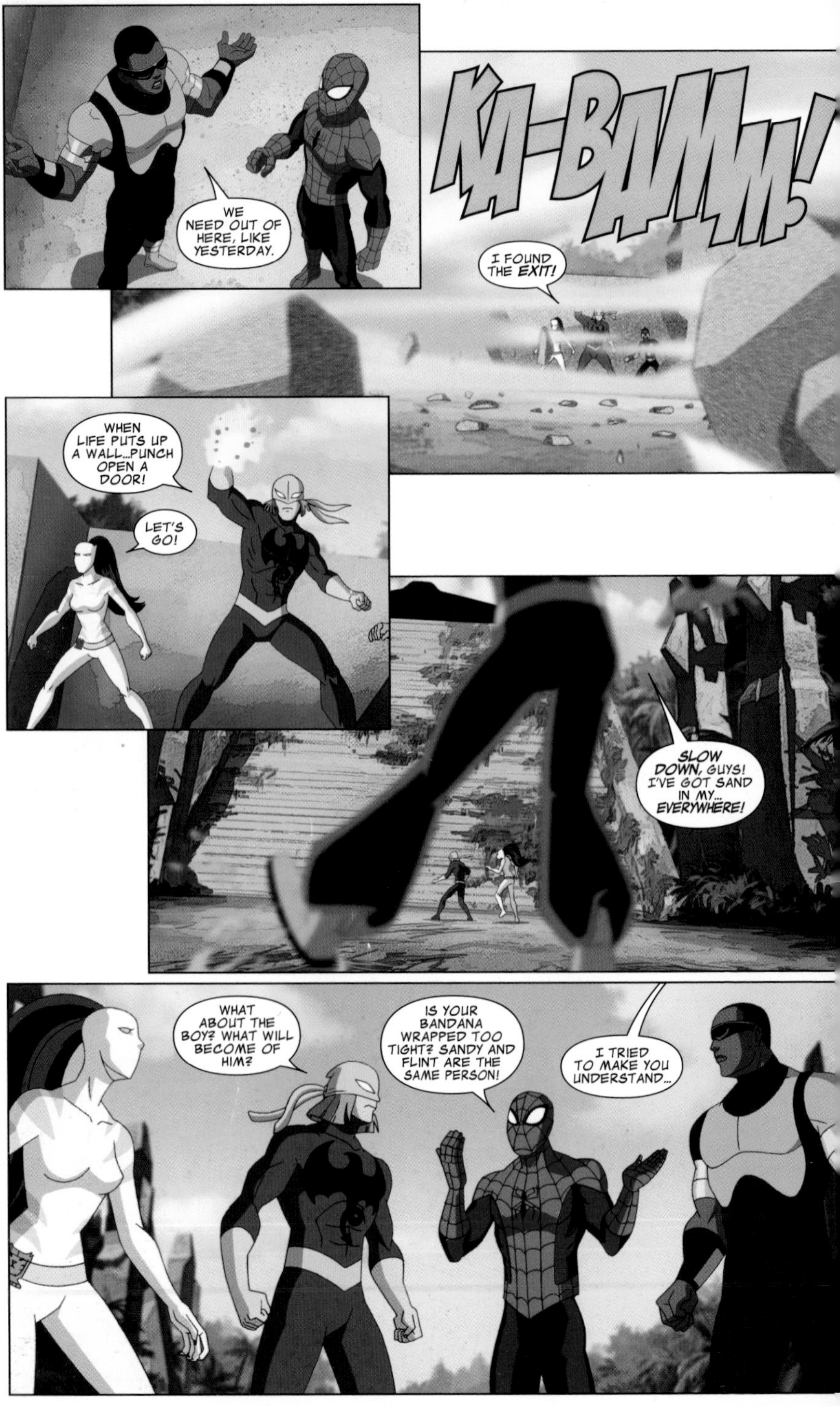

WE NEED OUT OF HERE, LIKE YESTERDAY.
KA-BAMM!
I FOUND THE EXIT!
WHEN LIFE PUTS UP A WALL...PUNCH OPEN A DOOR!
LET'S GO!
SLOW DOWN, GUYS! I'VE GOT SAND IN MY... EVERYWHERE!
WHAT ABOUT THE BOY? WHAT WILL BECOME OF HIM?
IS YOUR BANDANA WRAPPED TOO TIGHT? SANDY AND FLINT ARE THE SAME PERSON!
I TRIED TO MAKE YOU UNDERSTAND...

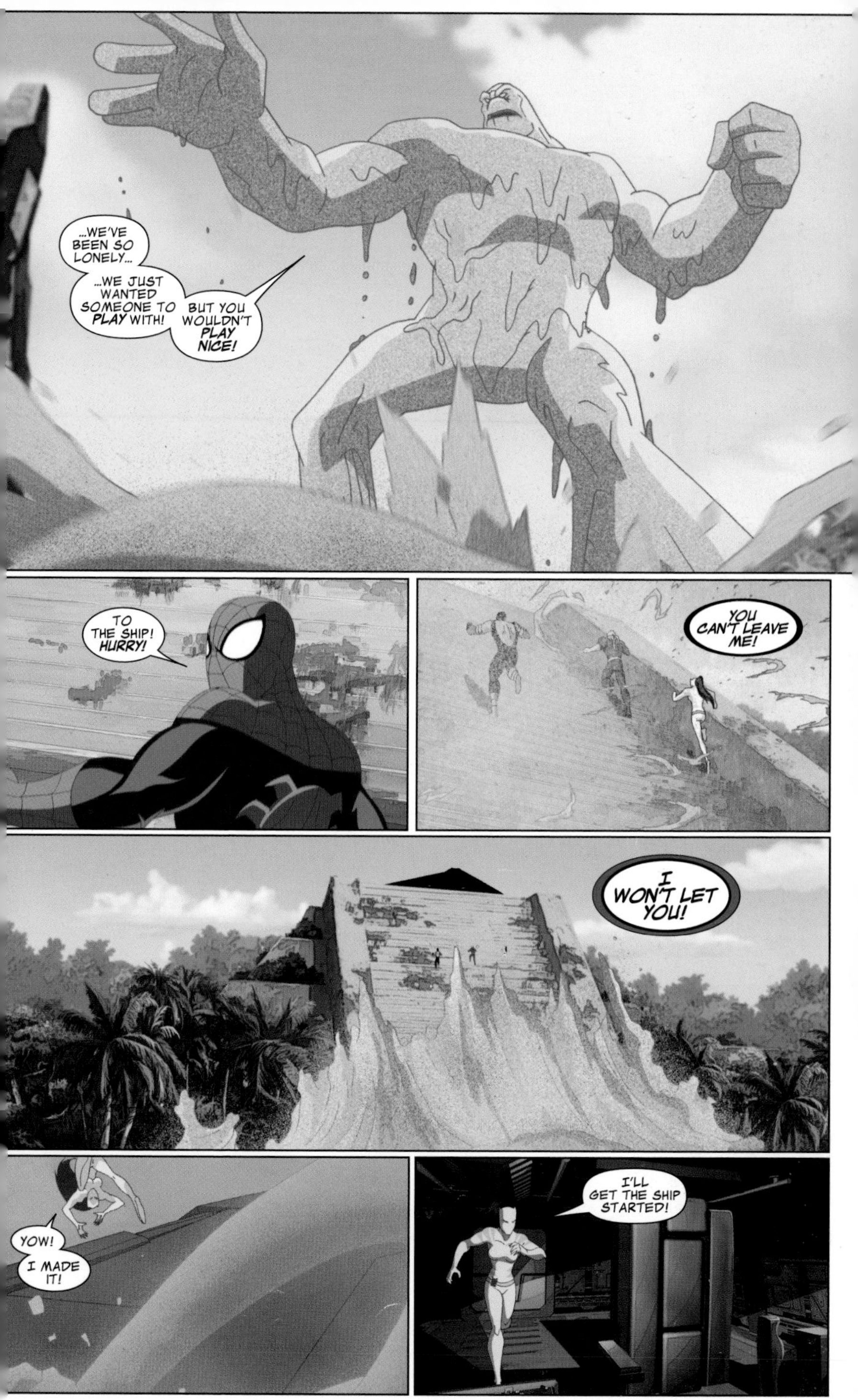
...WE'VE BEEN SO LONELY...
...WE JUST WANTED SOMEONE TO PLAY WITH!
BUT YOU WOULDN'T PLAY NICE!
TO THE SHIP! HURRY!
YOU CAN'T LEAVE ME!
I WON'T LET YOU!
YOW! I MADE IT!
I'LL GET THE SHIP STARTED!

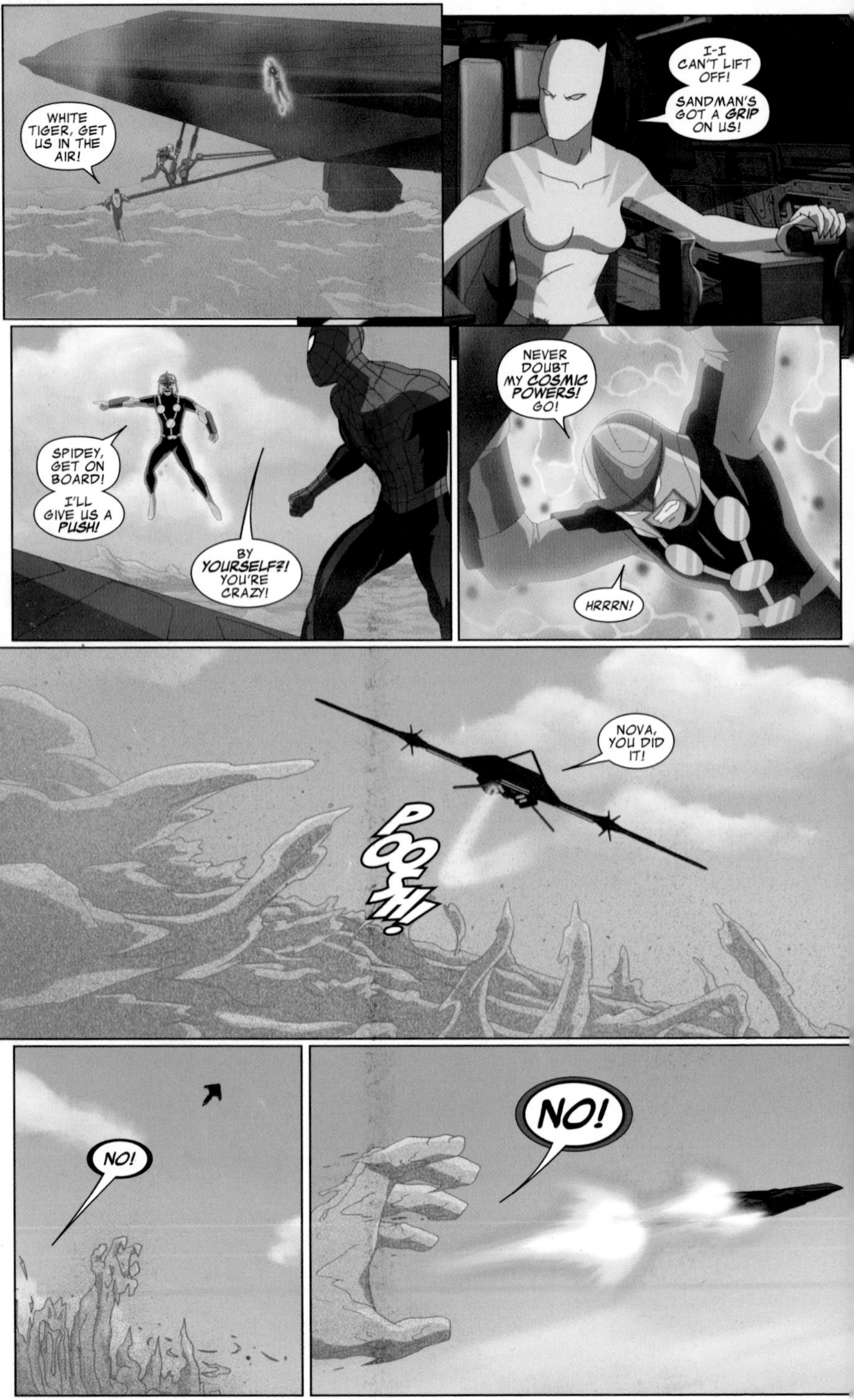
WHITE TIGER, GET US IN THE AIR!
I-I CAN'T LIFT OFF!
SANDMAN'S GOT A GRIP ON US!
SPIDEY, GET ON BOARD!
I'LL GIVE US A PUSH!
BY YOURSELF?! YOU'RE CRAZY!
NEVER DOUBT MY COSMIC POWERS! GO!
HRRRN!
NOVA, YOU DID IT!
POOOM!!
NO!
NO!

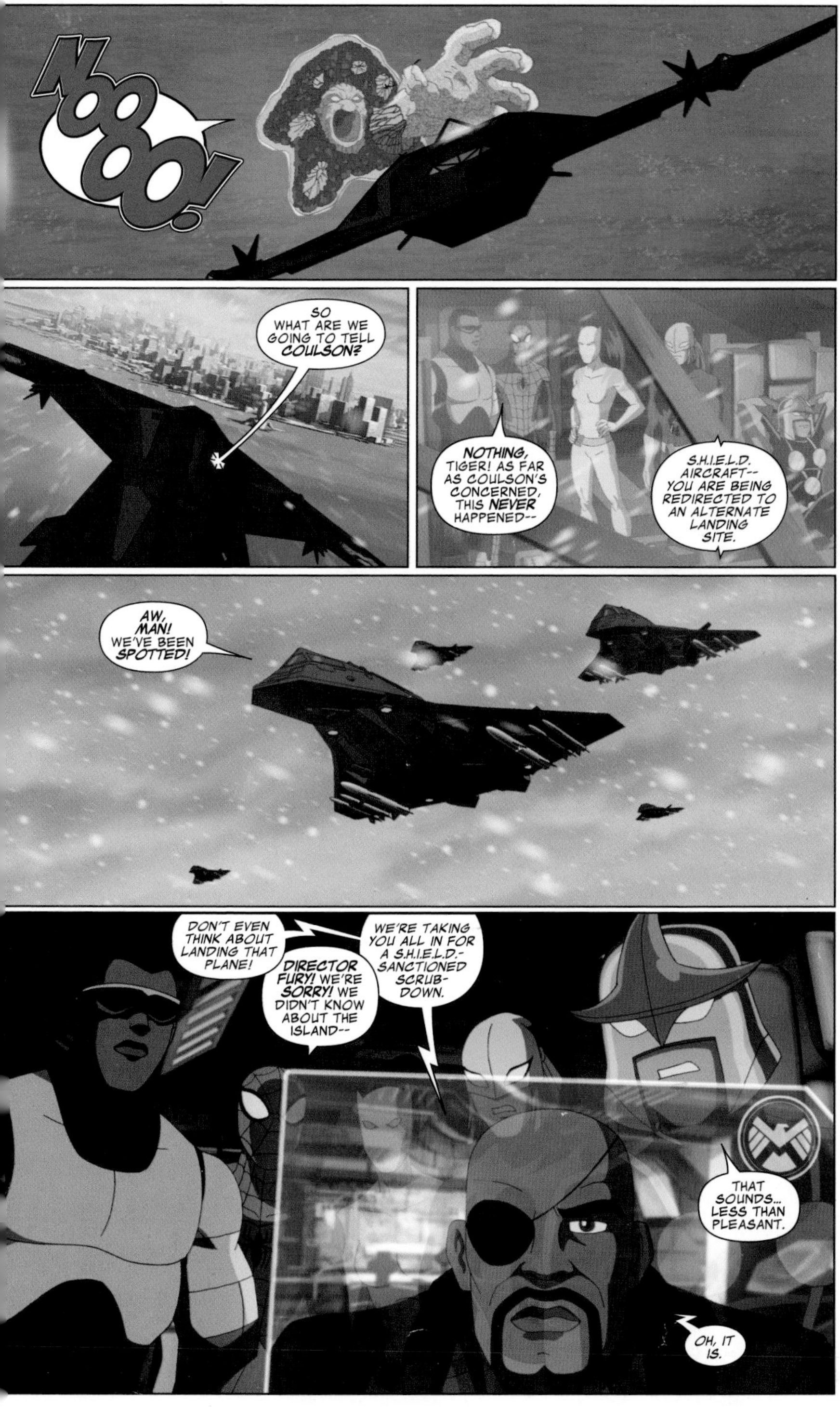

NOOOOO!
SO WHAT ARE WE GOING TO TELL COULSON?
NOTHING, TIGER! AS FAR AS COULSON'S CONCERNED, THIS NEVER HAPPENED--
S.H.I.E.L.D. AIRCRAFT-- YOU ARE BEING REDIRECTED TO AN ALTERNATE LANDING SITE.
AW, MAN! WE'VE BEEN SPOTTED!
DON'T EVEN THINK ABOUT LANDING THAT PLANE!
WE'RE TAKING YOU ALL IN FOR A S.H.I.E.L.D.-SANCTIONED SCRUB-DOWN.
DIRECTOR FURY! WE'RE SORRY! WE DIDN'T KNOW ABOUT THE ISLAND--
THAT SOUNDS... LESS THAN PLEASANT.
OH, IT IS.

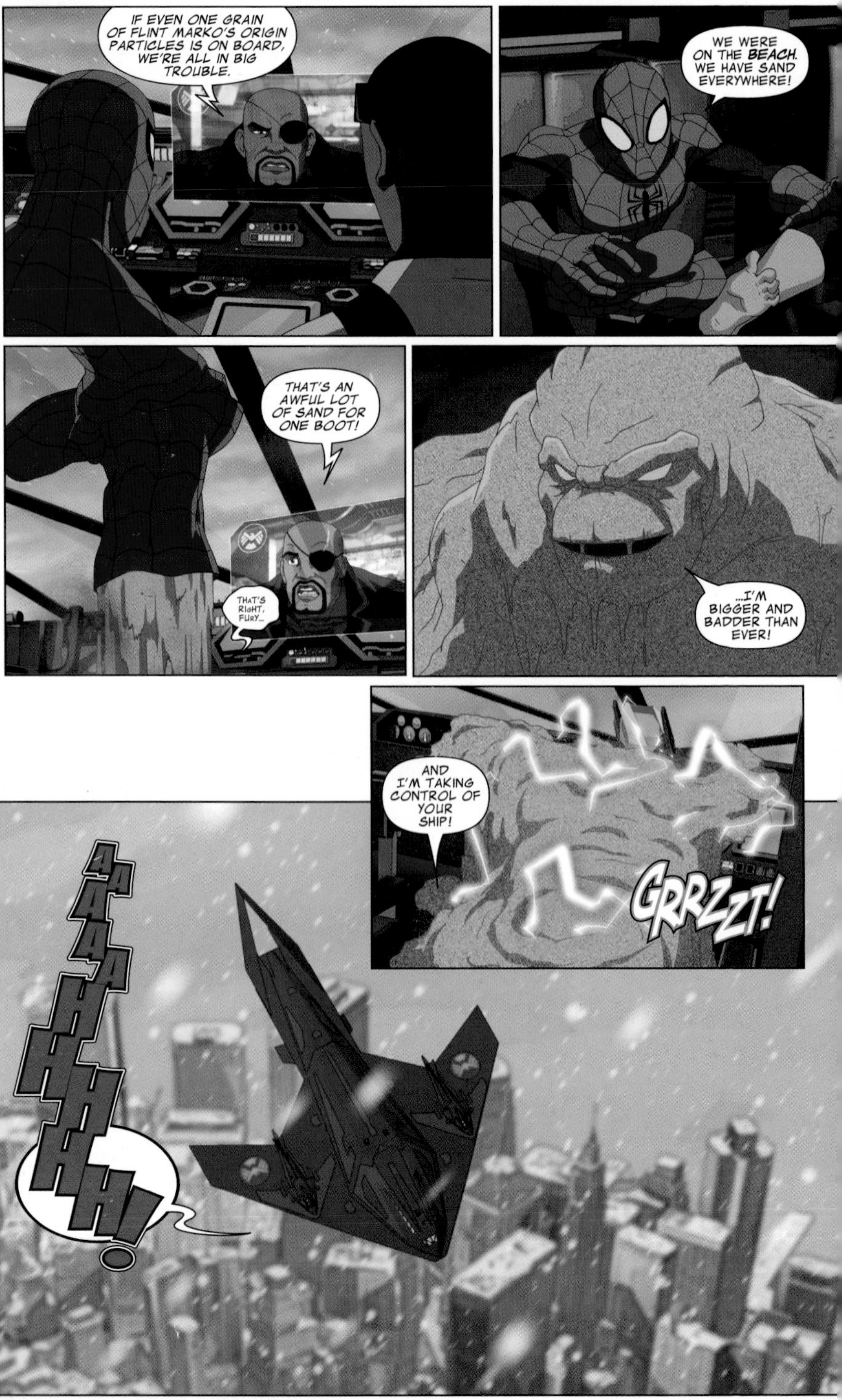
IF EVEN ONE GRAIN OF FLINT MARKO'S ORIGIN PARTICLES IS ON BOARD, WE'RE ALL IN BIG TROUBLE.
WE WERE ON THE BEACH. WE HAVE SAND EVERYWHERE!
THAT'S AN AWFUL LOT OF SAND FOR ONE BOOT!
THAT'S RIGHT, FURY...
...I'M BIGGER AND BADDER THAN EVER!
AND I'M TAKING CONTROL OF YOUR SHIP!
GRRZZT!
AAAAAHHHHHH!

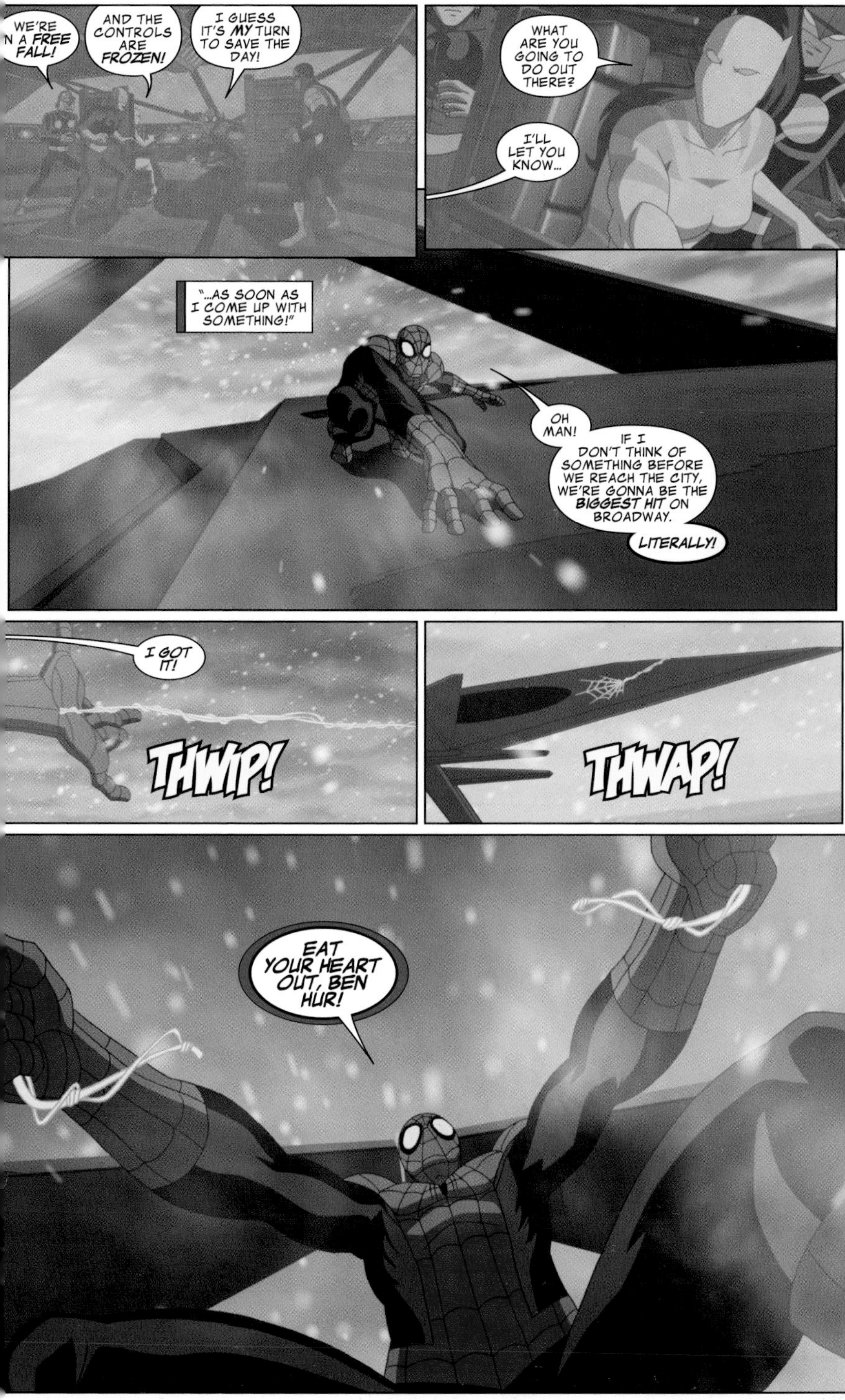

WE'RE N A FREE FALL!
AND THE CONTROLS ARE FROZEN!
I GUESS IT'S MY TURN TO SAVE THE DAY!
WHAT ARE YOU GOING TO DO OUT THERE?
I'LL LET YOU KNOW...
"...AS SOON AS I COME UP WITH SOMETHING!"
OH MAN!
IF I DON'T THINK OF SOMETHING BEFORE WE REACH THE CITY, WE'RE GONNA BE THE BIGGEST HIT ON BROADWAY.
LITERALLY!
I GOT IT!
THWIP!
THWAP!
EAT YOUR HEART OUT, BEN HUR!

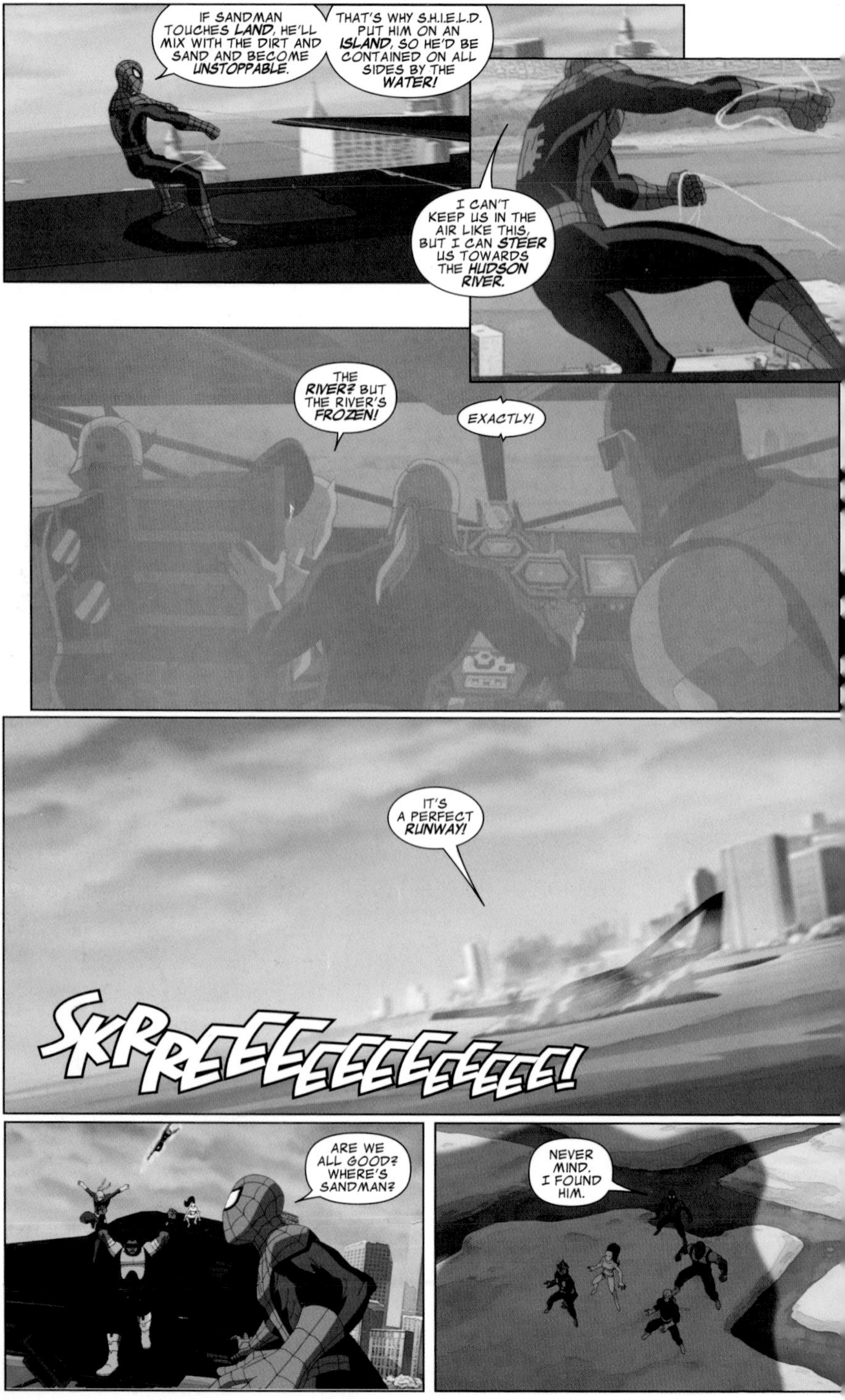
IF SANDMAN TOUCHES LAND, HE'LL MIX WITH THE DIRT AND SAND AND BECOME UNSTOPPABLE.
THAT'S WHY S.H.I.E.L.D. PUT HIM ON AN ISLAND, SO HE'D BE CONTAINED ON ALL SIDES BY THE WATER!
I CAN'T KEEP US IN THE AIR LIKE THIS, BUT I CAN STEER US TOWARDS THE HUDSON RIVER.
THE RIVER? BUT THE RIVER'S FROZEN!
EXACTLY!
IT'S A PERFECT RUNWAY!
SKRREEEEEEEEEEEEEEE!
ARE WE ALL GOOD? WHERE'S SANDMAN?
NEVER MIND. I FOUND HIM.

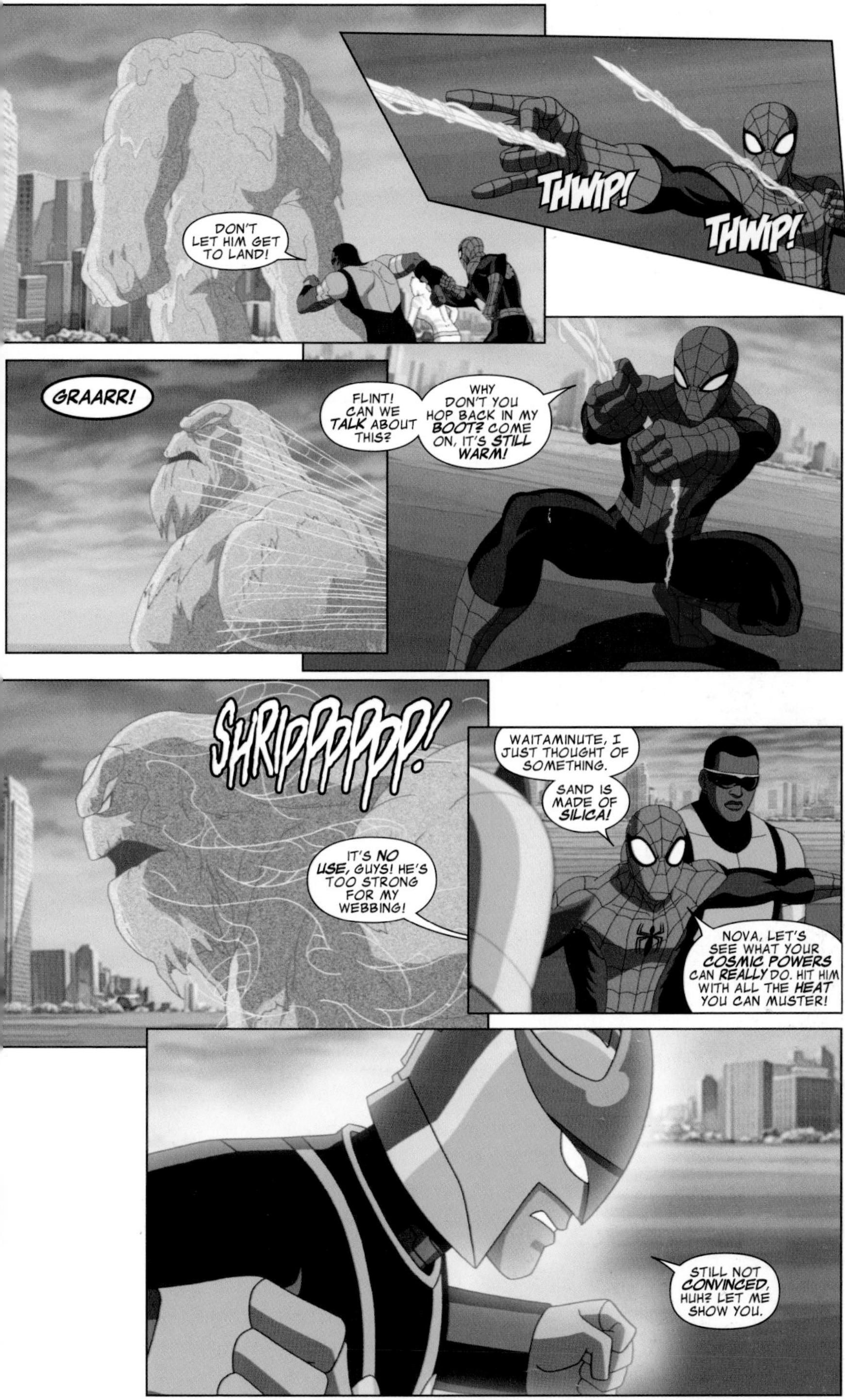
DON'T LET HIM GET TO LAND!
THWIP!
THWIP!
GRAARR!
FLINT! CAN WE TALK ABOUT THIS?
WHY DON'T YOU HOP BACK IN MY BOOT? COME ON, IT'S STILL WARM!
SHRIPPPPPP!
IT'S NO USE, GUYS! HE'S TOO STRONG FOR MY WEBBING!
WAITAMINUTE, I JUST THOUGHT OF SOMETHING.
SAND IS MADE OF SILICA!
NOVA, LET'S SEE WHAT YOUR COSMIC POWERS CAN REALLY DO. HIT HIM WITH ALL THE HEAT YOU CAN MUSTER!
STILL NOT CONVINCED, HUH? LET ME SHOW YOU.

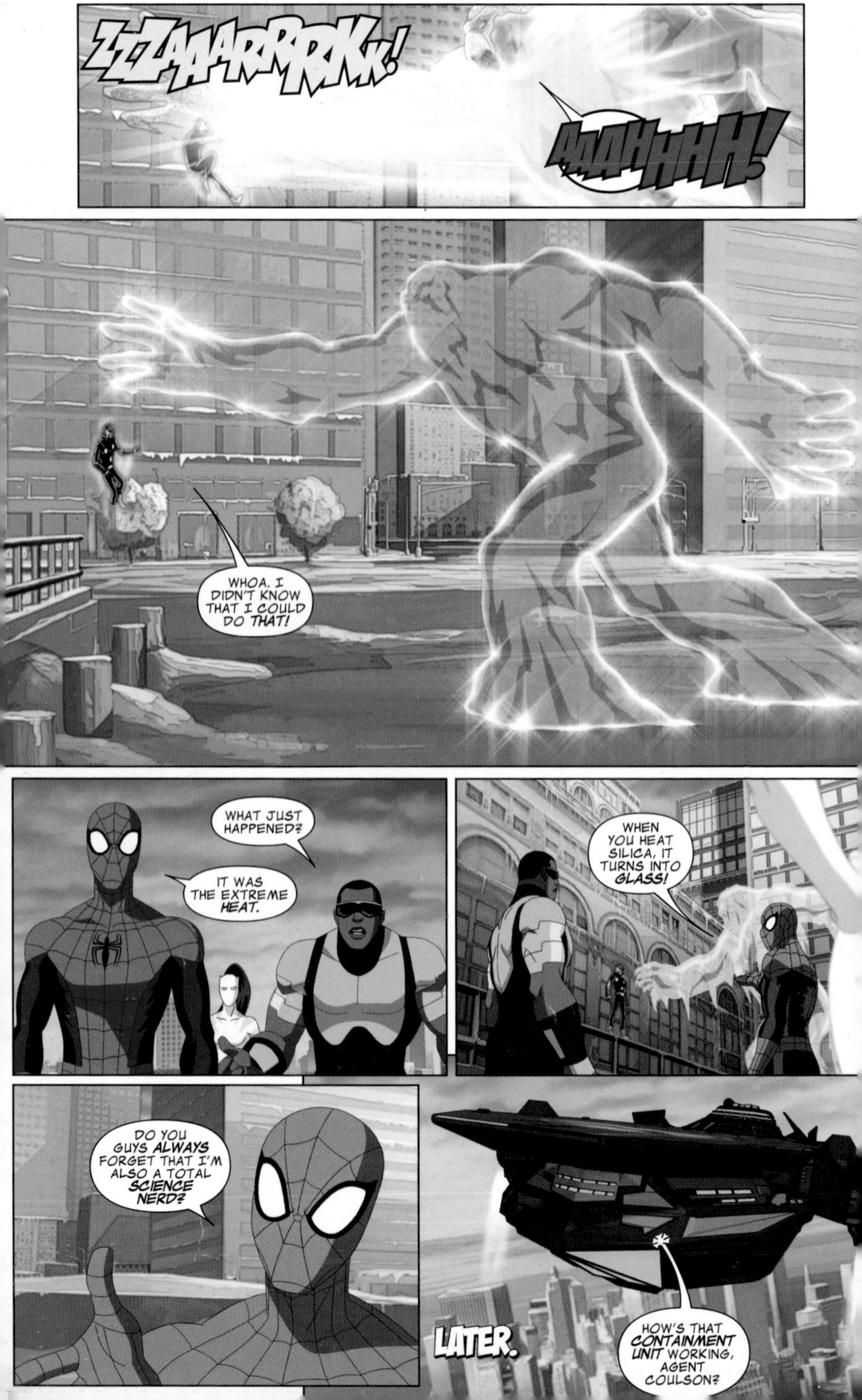
ZZZAAARRRRKKK!
AAAHHHH!
WHOA. I DIDN'T KNOW THAT I COULD DO THAT!
WHAT JUST HAPPENED?
IT WAS THE EXTREME HEAT.
WHEN YOU HEAT SILICA, IT TURNS INTO GLASS!
DO YOU GUYS ALWAYS FORGET THAT I'M ALSO A TOTAL SCIENCE NERD?
LATER.
HOW'S THAT CONTAINMENT UNIT WORKING, AGENT COULSON?

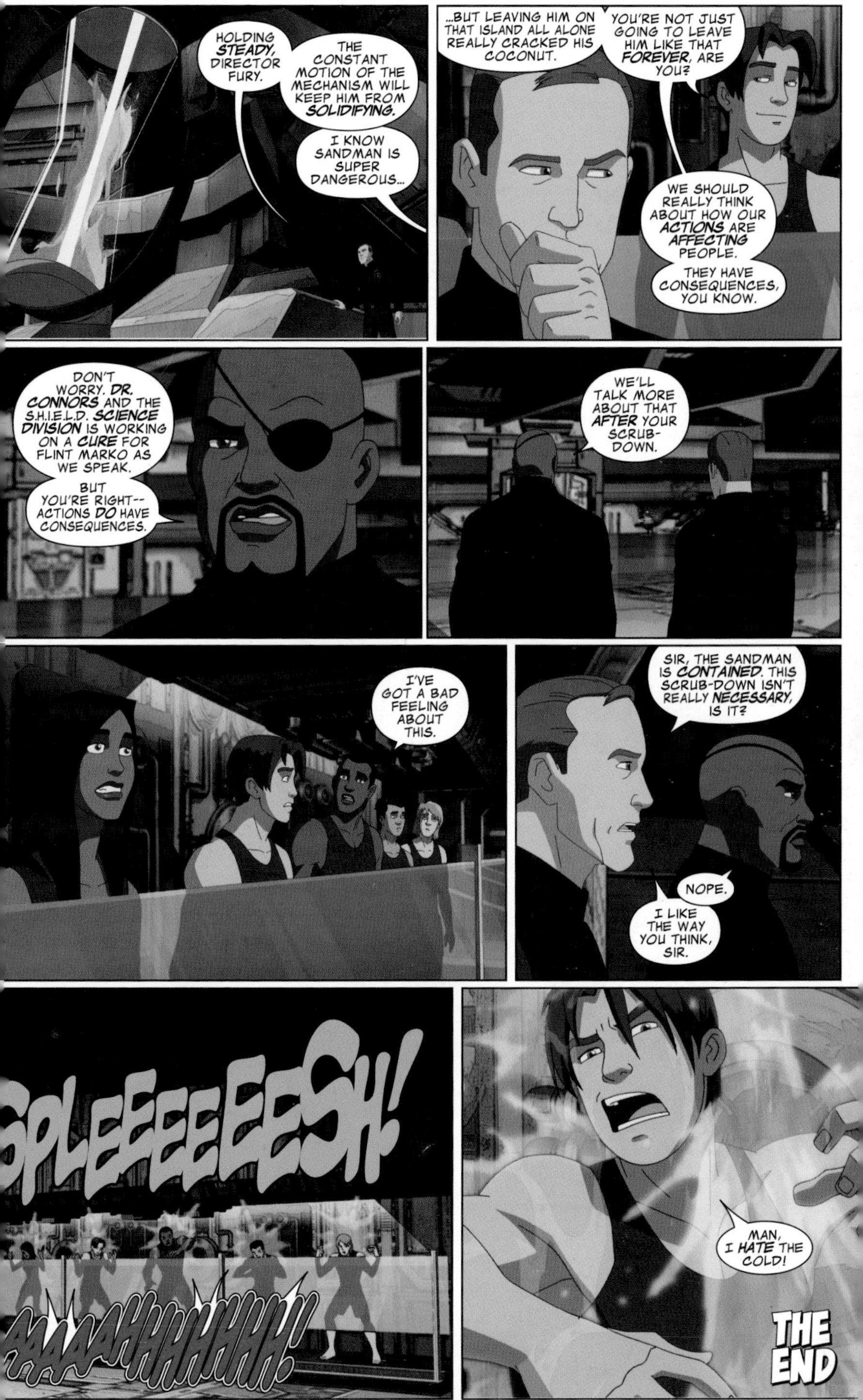
HOLDING STEADY, DIRECTOR FURY.
THE CONSTANT MOTION OF THE MECHANISM WILL KEEP HIM FROM SOLIDIFYING.
I KNOW SANDMAN IS SUPER DANGEROUS...
...BUT LEAVING HIM ON THAT ISLAND ALL ALONE REALLY CRACKED HIS COCONUT.
YOU'RE NOT JUST GOING TO LEAVE HIM LIKE THAT FOREVER, ARE YOU?
WE SHOULD REALLY THINK ABOUT HOW OUR ACTIONS ARE AFFECTING PEOPLE.
THEY HAVE CONSEQUENCES, YOU KNOW.
DON'T WORRY. DR. CONNORS AND THE S.H.I.E.L.D. SCIENCE DIVISION IS WORKING ON A CURE FOR FLINT MARKO AS WE SPEAK.
BUT YOU'RE RIGHT-- ACTIONS DO HAVE CONSEQUENCES.
WE'LL TALK MORE ABOUT THAT AFTER YOUR SCRUB-DOWN.
I'VE GOT A BAD FEELING ABOUT THIS.
SIR, THE SANDMAN IS CONTAINED. THIS SCRUB-DOWN ISN'T REALLY NECESSARY, IS IT?
NOPE.
I LIKE THE WAY YOU THINK, SIR.
SPLEEEEEEESH!
AAAAAHHHHHHH!
MAN, I HATE THE COLD!
THE END

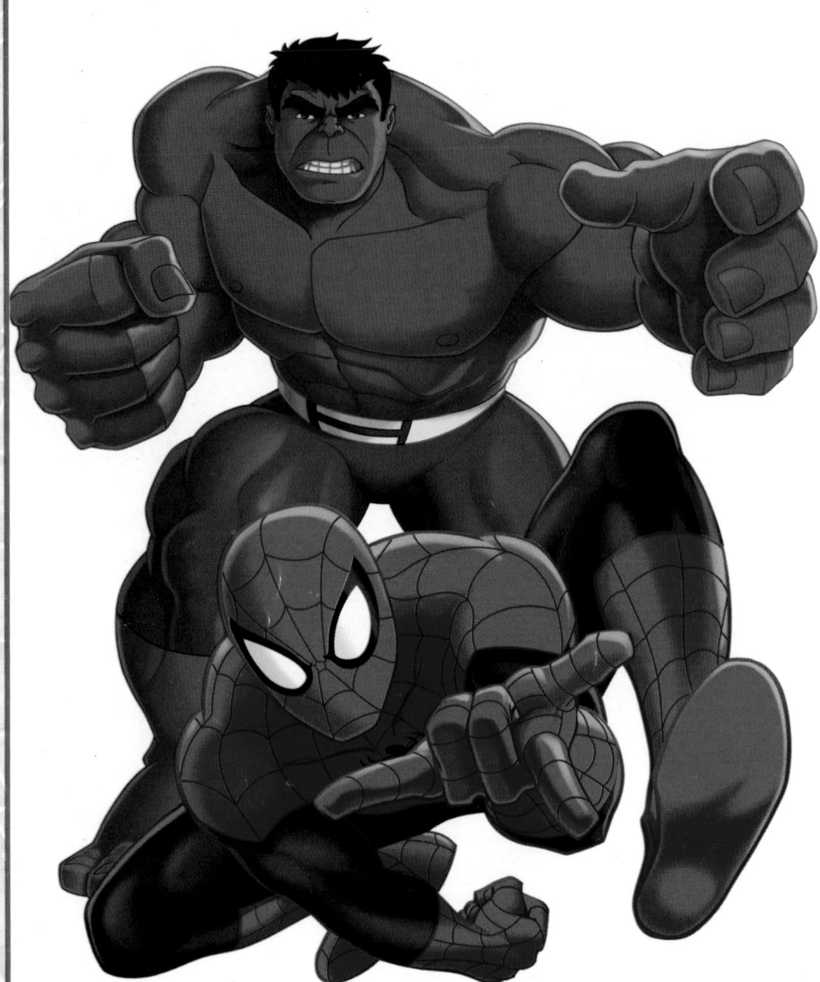

28

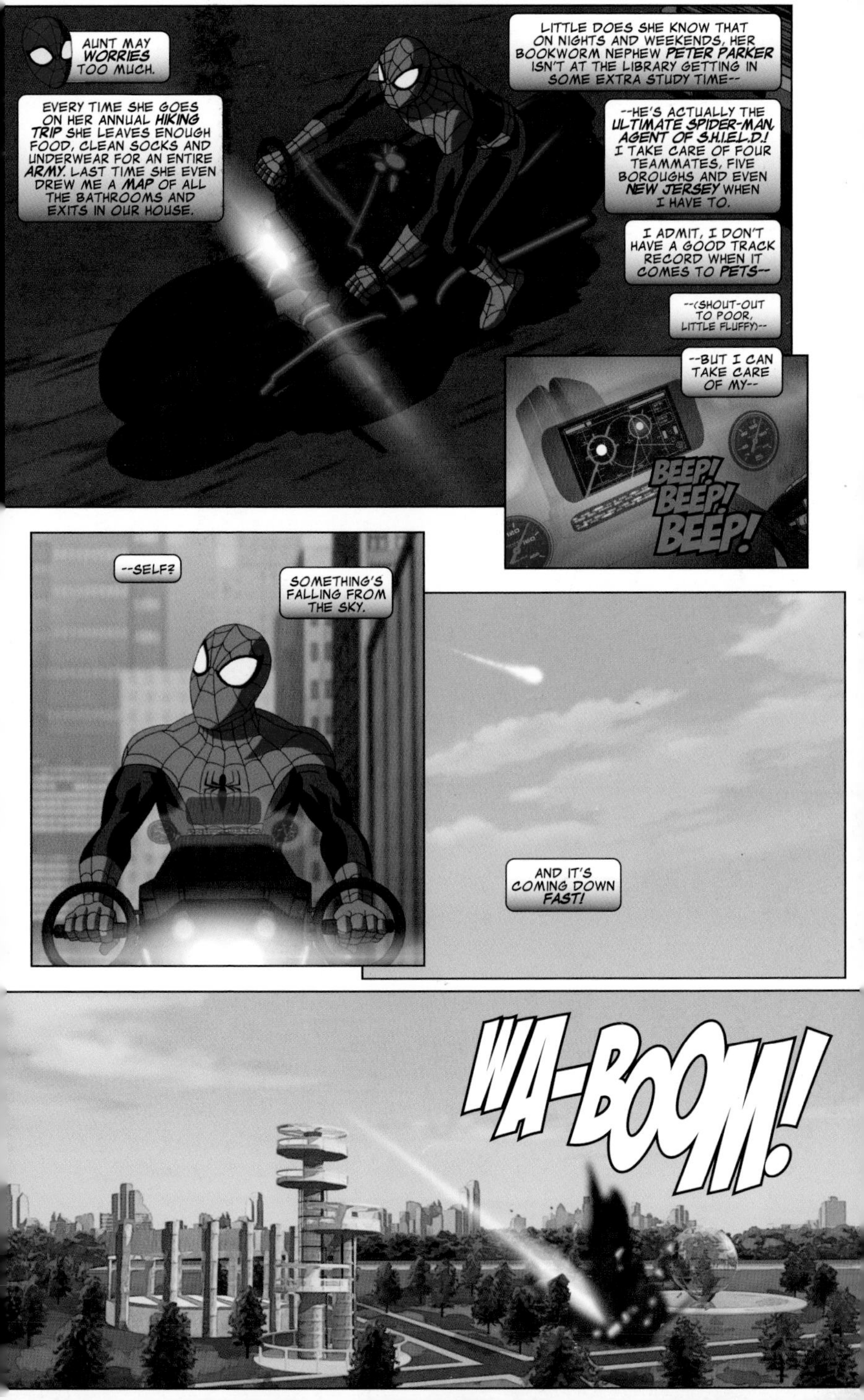
AUNT MAY WORRIES TOO MUCH.
EVERY TIME SHE GOES ON HER ANNUAL HIKING TRIP SHE LEAVES ENOUGH FOOD, CLEAN SOCKS AND UNDERWEAR FOR AN ENTIRE ARMY. LAST TIME SHE EVEN DREW ME A MAP OF ALL THE BATHROOMS AND EXITS IN OUR HOUSE.
LITTLE DOES SHE KNOW THAT ON NIGHTS AND WEEKENDS, HER BOOKWORM NEPHEW PETER PARKER ISN'T AT THE LIBRARY GETTING IN SOME EXTRA STUDY TIME--
--HE'S ACTUALLY THE ULTIMATE SPIDER-MAN, AGENT OF S.H.I.E.L.D.! I TAKE CARE OF FOUR TEAMMATES, FIVE BOROUGHS AND EVEN NEW JERSEY WHEN I HAVE TO.
I ADMIT, I DON'T HAVE A GOOD TRACK RECORD WHEN IT COMES TO PETS--
--(SHOUT-OUT TO POOR, LITTLE FLUFFY)--
--BUT I CAN TAKE CARE OF MY--
BEEP! BEEP! BEEP!
--SELF?
SOMETHING'S FALLING FROM THE SKY.
AND IT'S COMING DOWN FAST!
WA-BOOM!

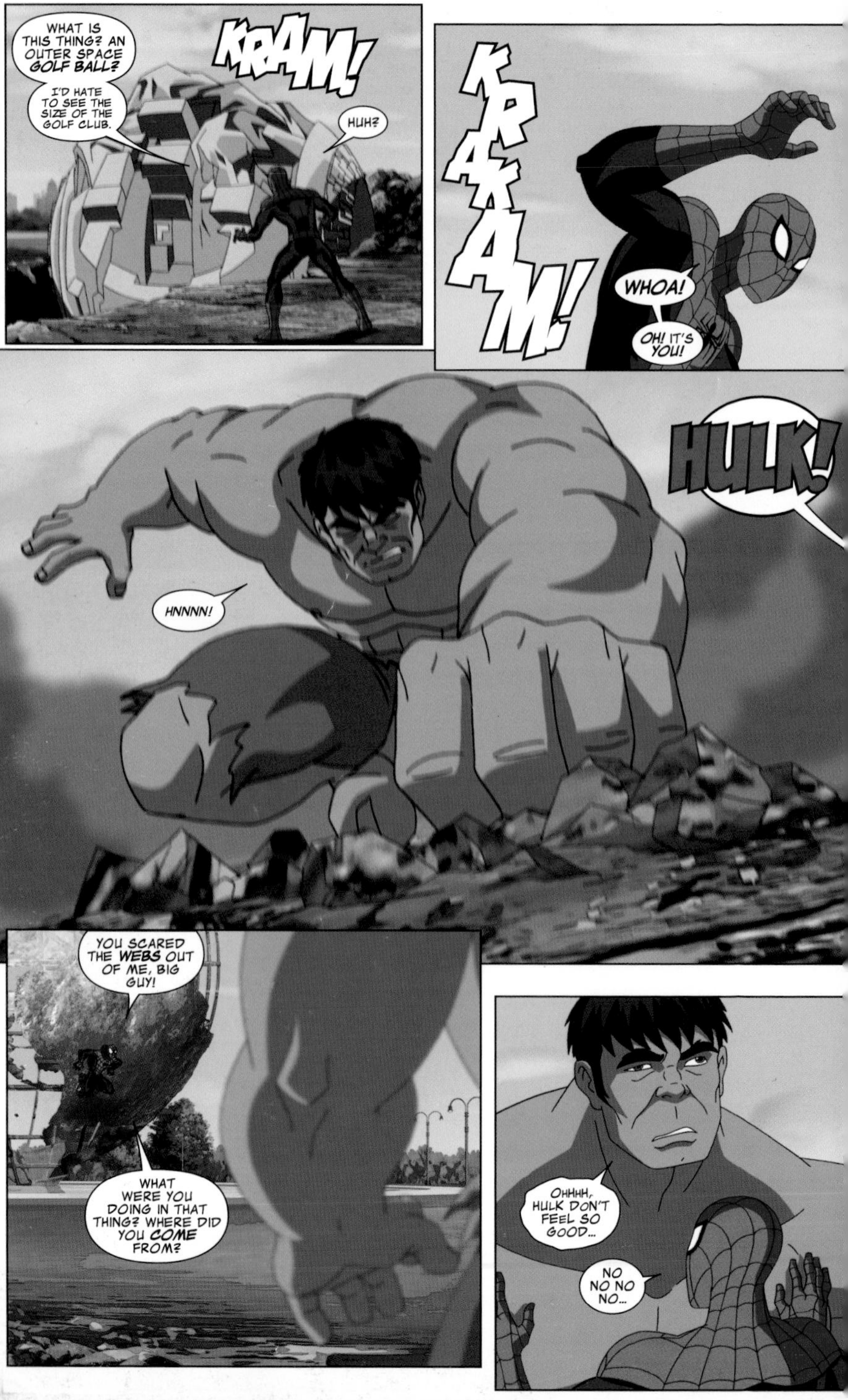
WHAT IS THIS THING? AN OUTER SPACE GOLF BALL?
I'D HATE TO SEE THE SIZE OF THE GOLF CLUB.
KRAM!
HUH?
KRAKAAM!
WHOA!
OH! IT'S YOU!
HULK!
HNNNN!
YOU SCARED THE WEBS OUT OF ME, BIG GUY!
WHAT WERE YOU DOING IN THAT THING? WHERE DID YOU COME FROM?
OHHHH, HULK DON'T FEEL SO GOOD...
NO NO NO NO...

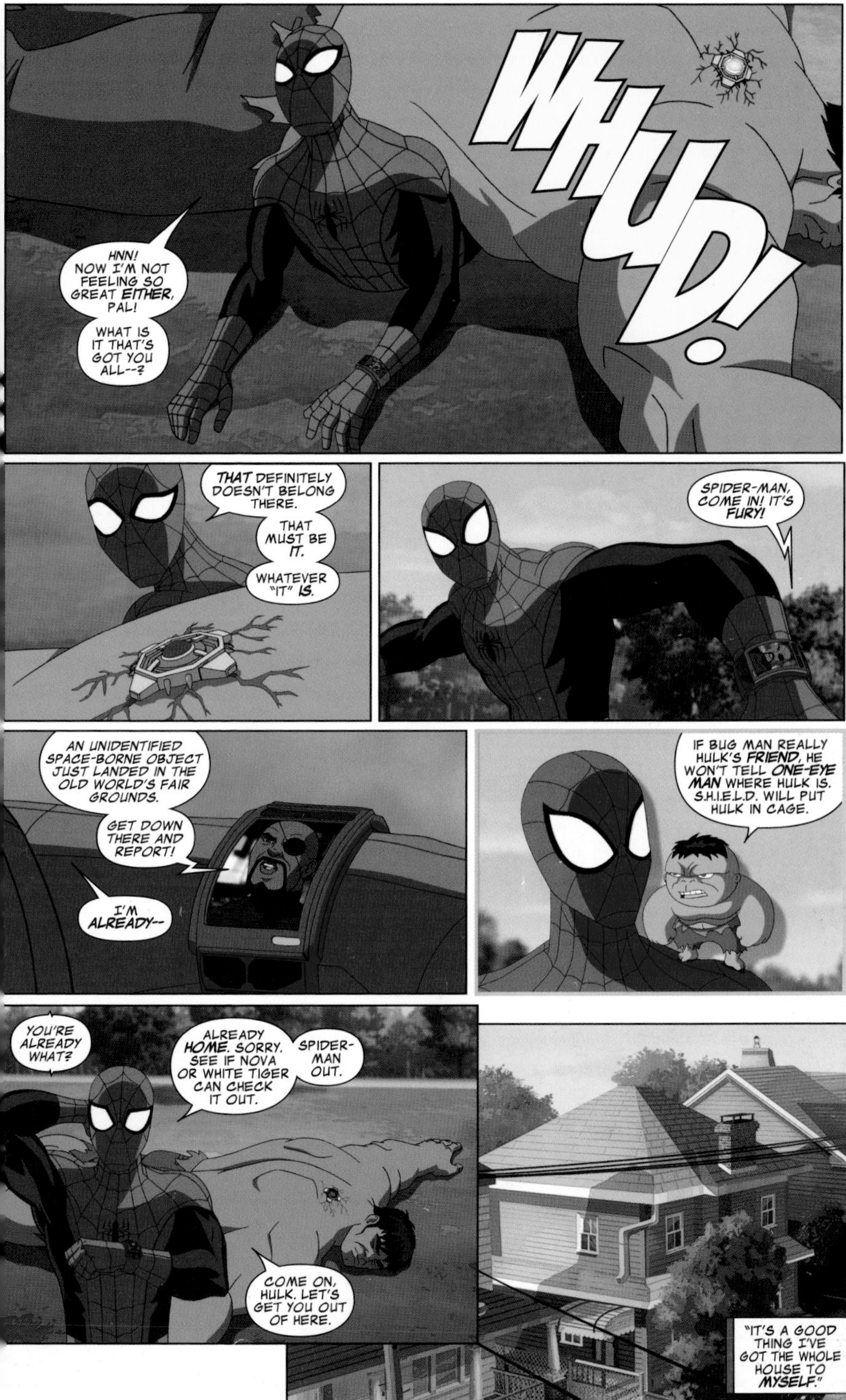

WHUD!
HNN! NOW I'M NOT FEELING SO GREAT EITHER, PAL!
WHAT IS IT THAT'S GOT YOU ALL--?
THAT DEFINITELY DOESN'T BELONG THERE.
THAT MUST BE IT.
WHATEVER "IT" IS.
SPIDER-MAN, COME IN! IT'S FURY!
AN UNIDENTIFIED SPACE-BORNE OBJECT JUST LANDED IN THE OLD WORLD'S FAIR GROUNDS.
GET DOWN THERE AND REPORT!
I'M ALREADY--
IF BUG MAN REALLY HULK'S FRIEND, HE WON'T TELL ONE-EYE MAN WHERE HULK IS. S.H.I.E.L.D. WILL PUT HULK IN CAGE.
YOU'RE ALREADY WHAT?
ALREADY HOME. SORRY. SEE IF NOVA OR WHITE TIGER CAN CHECK IT OUT.
SPIDER-MAN OUT.
COME ON, HULK. LET'S GET YOU OUT OF HERE.
"IT'S A GOOD THING I'VE GOT THE WHOLE HOUSE TO MYSELF."

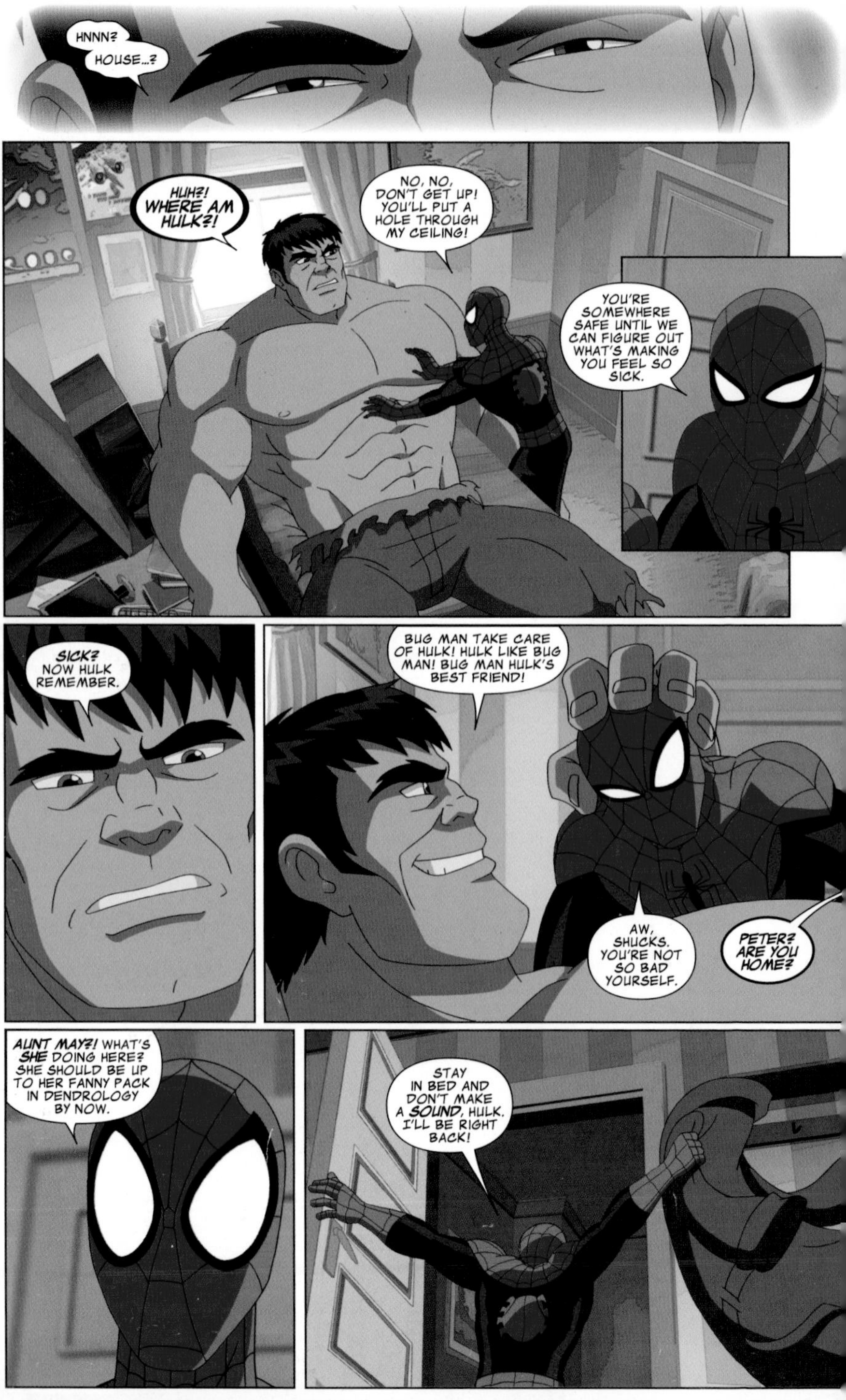
HNNN?
HOUSE...?
HUH?! WHERE AM HULK?!
NO, NO, DON'T GET UP! YOU'LL PUT A HOLE THROUGH MY CEILING!
YOU'RE SOMEWHERE SAFE UNTIL WE CAN FIGURE OUT WHAT'S MAKING YOU FEEL SO SICK.
SICK? NOW HULK REMEMBER.
BUG MAN TAKE CARE OF HULK! HULK LIKE BUG MAN! BUG MAN HULK'S BEST FRIEND!
AW, SHUCKS. YOU'RE NOT SO BAD YOURSELF.
PETER? ARE YOU HOME?
AUNT MAY?! WHAT'S SHE DOING HERE? SHE SHOULD BE UP TO HER FANNY PACK IN DENDROLOGY BY NOW.
STAY IN BED AND DON'T MAKE A SOUND, HULK. I'LL BE RIGHT BACK!

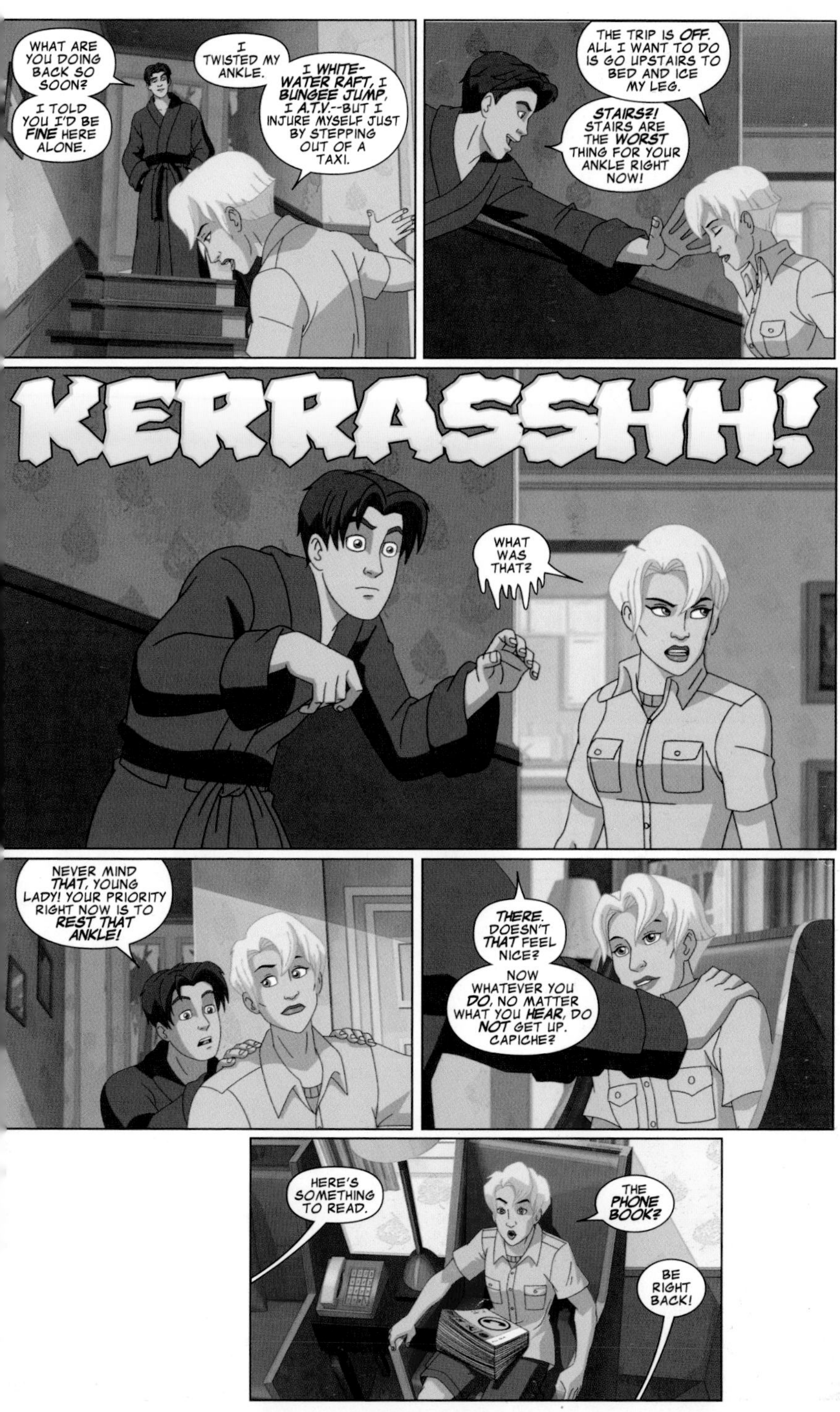
WHAT ARE YOU DOING BACK SO SOON?
I TOLD YOU I'D BE FINE HERE ALONE.
I TWISTED MY ANKLE.
I WHITE-WATER RAFT, I BUNGEE JUMP, I A.T.V.--BUT I INJURE MYSELF JUST BY STEPPING OUT OF A TAXI.
THE TRIP IS OFF. ALL I WANT TO DO IS GO UPSTAIRS TO BED AND ICE MY LEG.
STAIRS?! STAIRS ARE THE WORST THING FOR YOUR ANKLE RIGHT NOW!
KERRASSHH!
WHAT WAS THAT?
NEVER MIND THAT, YOUNG LADY! YOUR PRIORITY RIGHT NOW IS TO REST THAT ANKLE!
THERE. DOESN'T THAT FEEL NICE?
NOW WHATEVER YOU DO, NO MATTER WHAT YOU HEAR, DO NOT GET UP. CAPICHE?
HERE'S SOMETHING TO READ.
THE PHONE BOOK?
BE RIGHT BACK!

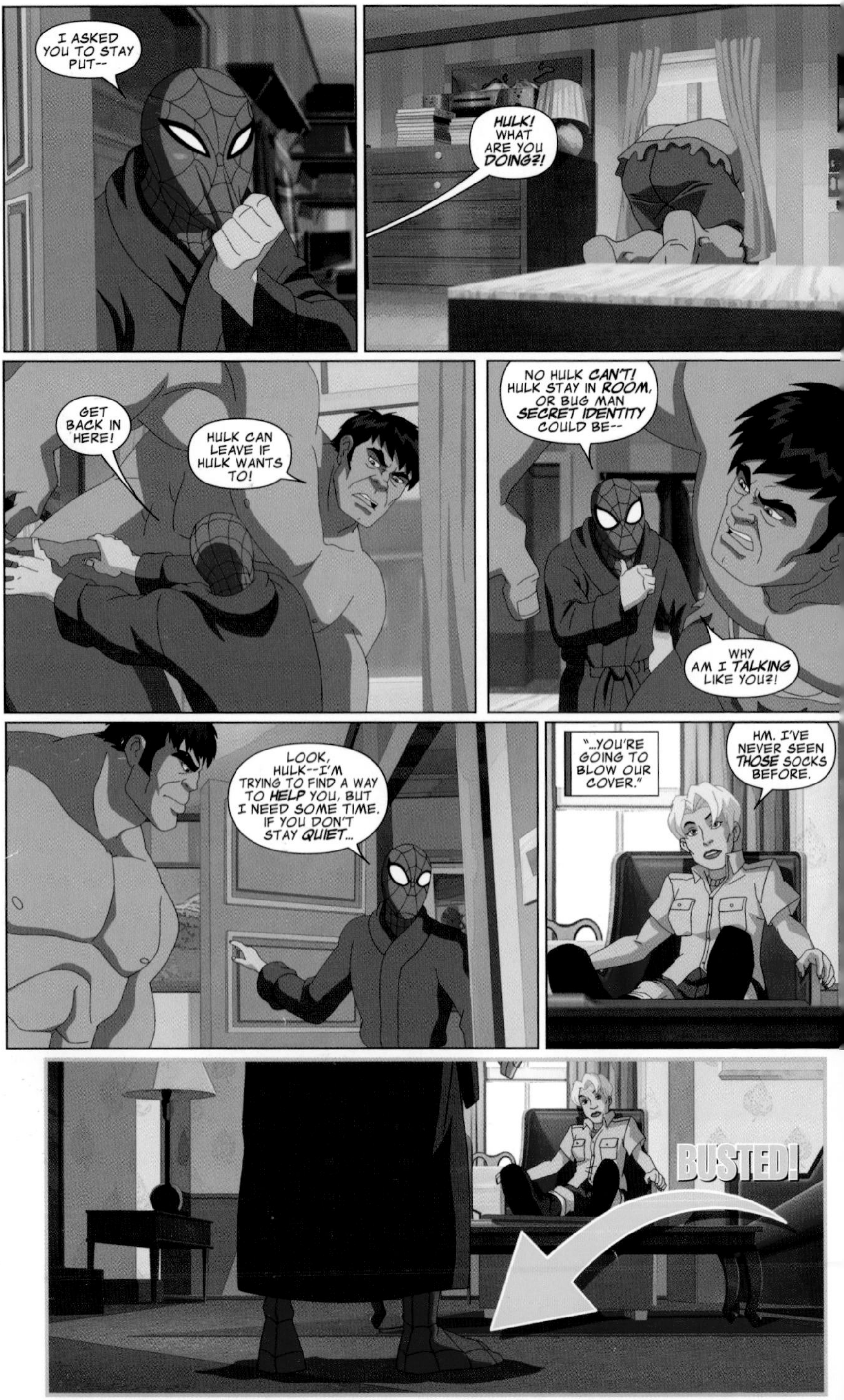

I ASKED YOU TO STAY PUT--
HULK! WHAT ARE YOU DOING?!
GET BACK IN HERE!
HULK CAN LEAVE IF HULK WANTS TO!
NO HULK CAN'T! HULK STAY IN ROOM, OR BUG MAN SECRET IDENTITY COULD BE--
WHY AM I TALKING LIKE YOU?!
LOOK, HULK--I'M TRYING TO FIND A WAY TO HELP YOU, BUT I NEED SOME TIME. IF YOU DON'T STAY QUIET...
"...YOU'RE GOING TO BLOW OUR COVER."
HM. I'VE NEVER SEEN THOSE SOCKS BEFORE.
BUSTED!

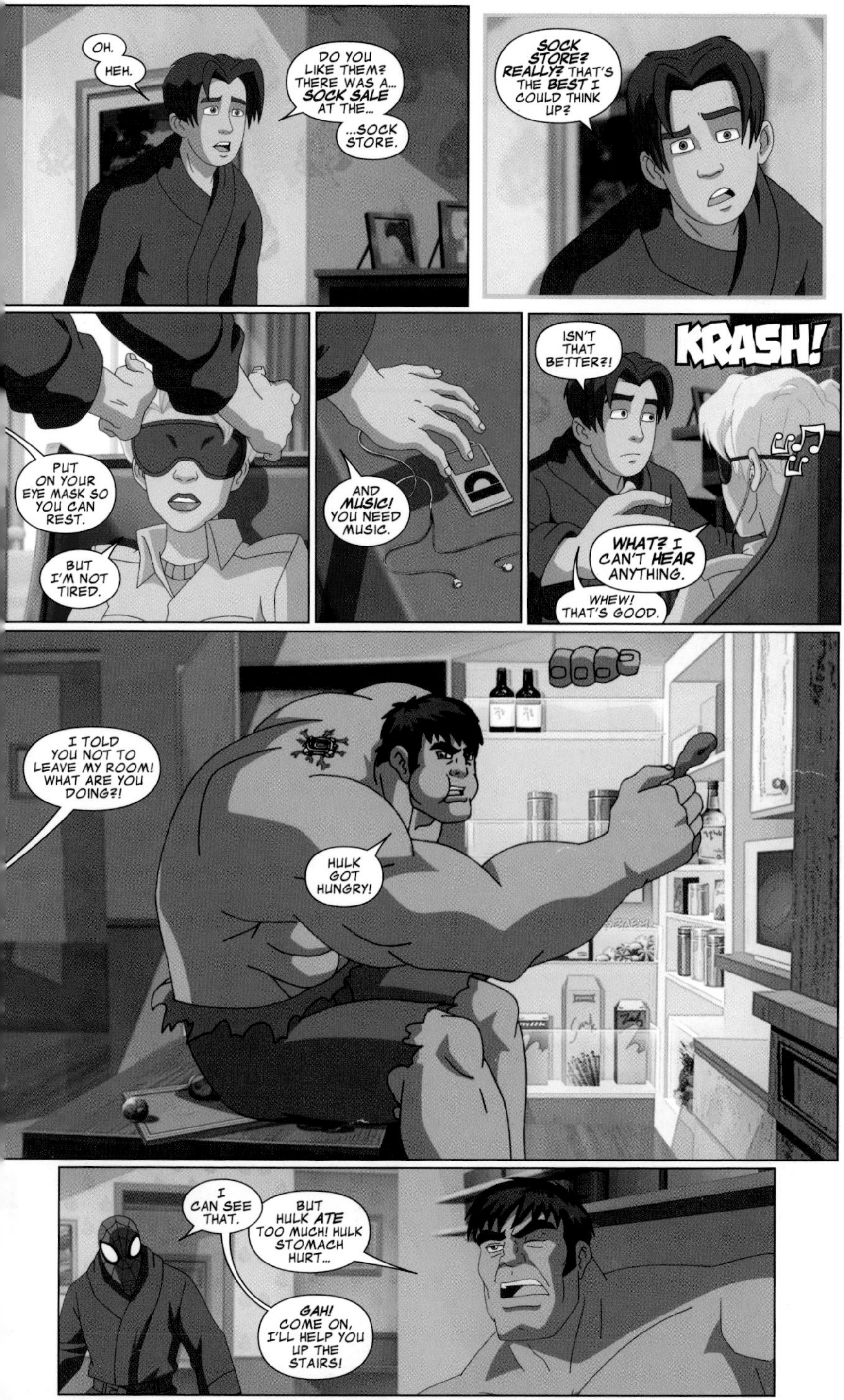

OH.
HEH.
DO YOU LIKE THEM? THERE WAS A... SOCK SALE AT THE...
...SOCK STORE.
SOCK STORE? REALLY? THAT'S THE BEST I COULD THINK UP?
PUT ON YOUR EYE MASK SO YOU CAN REST.
BUT I'M NOT TIRED.
AND MUSIC! YOU NEED MUSIC.
ISN'T THAT BETTER?!
KRASH!
WHAT? I CAN'T HEAR ANYTHING.
WHEW! THAT'S GOOD.
I TOLD YOU NOT TO LEAVE MY ROOM! WHAT ARE YOU DOING?!
HULK GOT HUNGRY!
I CAN SEE THAT.
BUT HULK ATE TOO MUCH! HULK STOMACH HURT...
GAH! COME ON, I'LL HELP YOU UP THE STAIRS!

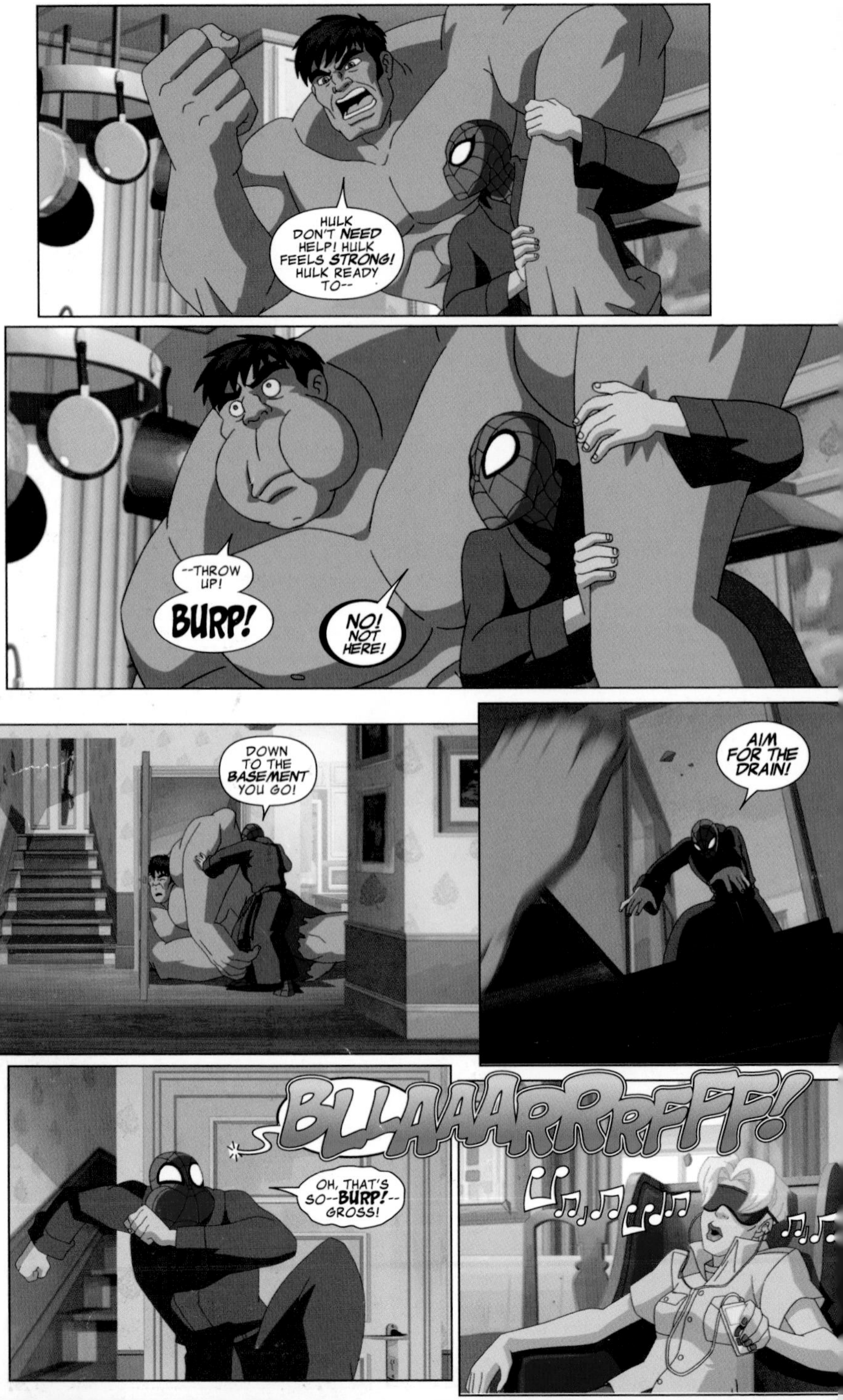
HULK DON'T NEED HELP! HULK FEELS STRONG! HULK READY TO--
--THROW UP!
BURP!
NO! NOT HERE!
DOWN TO THE BASEMENT YOU GO!
AIM FOR THE DRAIN!
BLLAAARRRRFFFF!
OH, THAT'S SO--BURP!--GROSS!

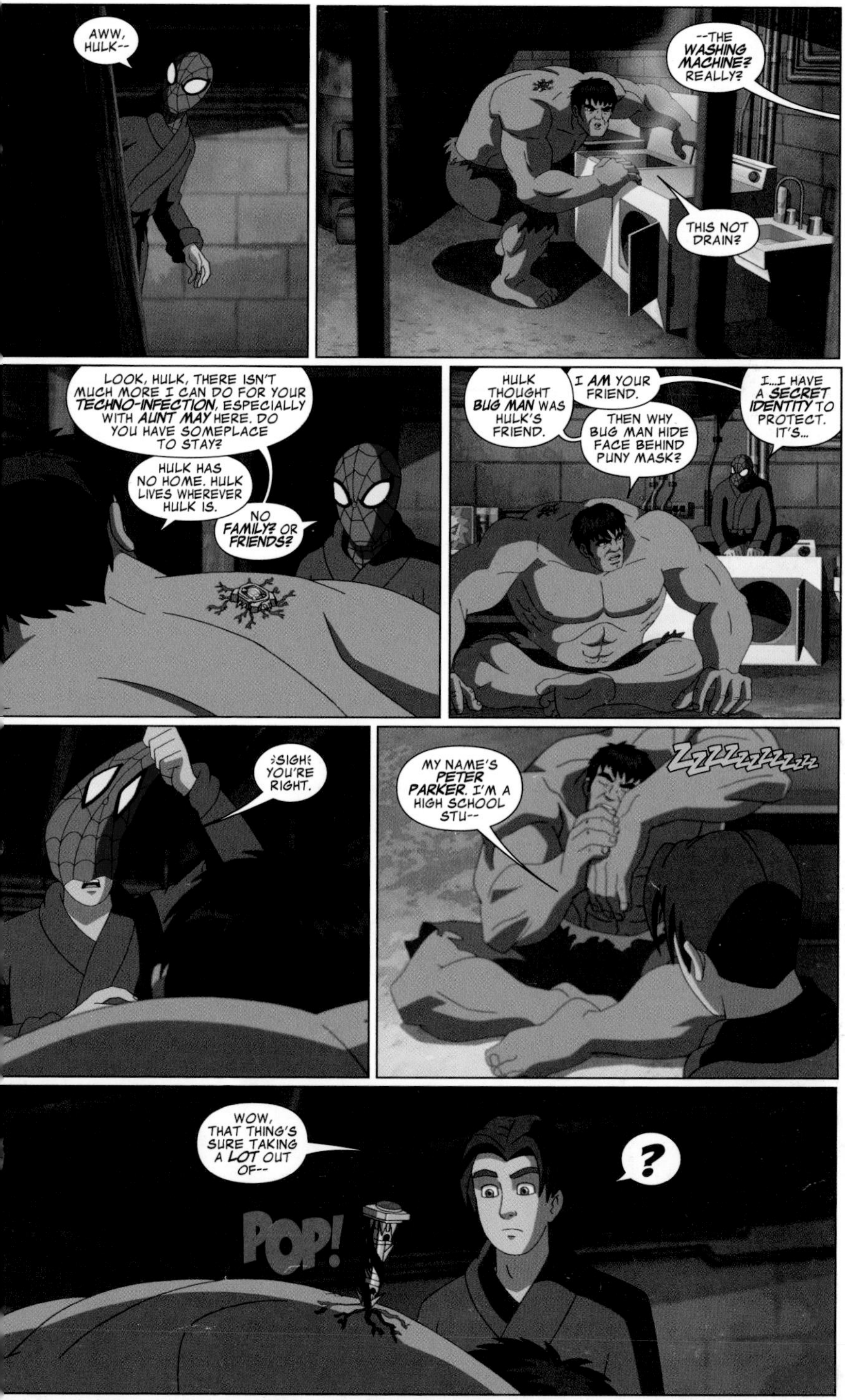

AWW, HULK--
--THE WASHING MACHINE? REALLY?
THIS NOT DRAIN?
LOOK, HULK, THERE ISN'T MUCH MORE I CAN DO FOR YOUR TECHNO-INFECTION, ESPECIALLY WITH AUNT MAY HERE. DO YOU HAVE SOMEPLACE TO STAY?
HULK HAS NO HOME. HULK LIVES WHEREVER HULK IS.
NO FAMILY? OR FRIENDS?
HULK THOUGHT BUG MAN WAS HULK'S FRIEND.
I AM YOUR FRIEND.
THEN WHY BUG MAN HIDE FACE BEHIND PUNY MASK?
I...I HAVE A SECRET IDENTITY TO PROTECT. IT'S...
SIGH YOU'RE RIGHT.
MY NAME'S PETER PARKER. I'M A HIGH SCHOOL STU--
ZZZZZZZZZZZZ
WOW, THAT THING'S SURE TAKING A LOT OUT OF--
?
POP!

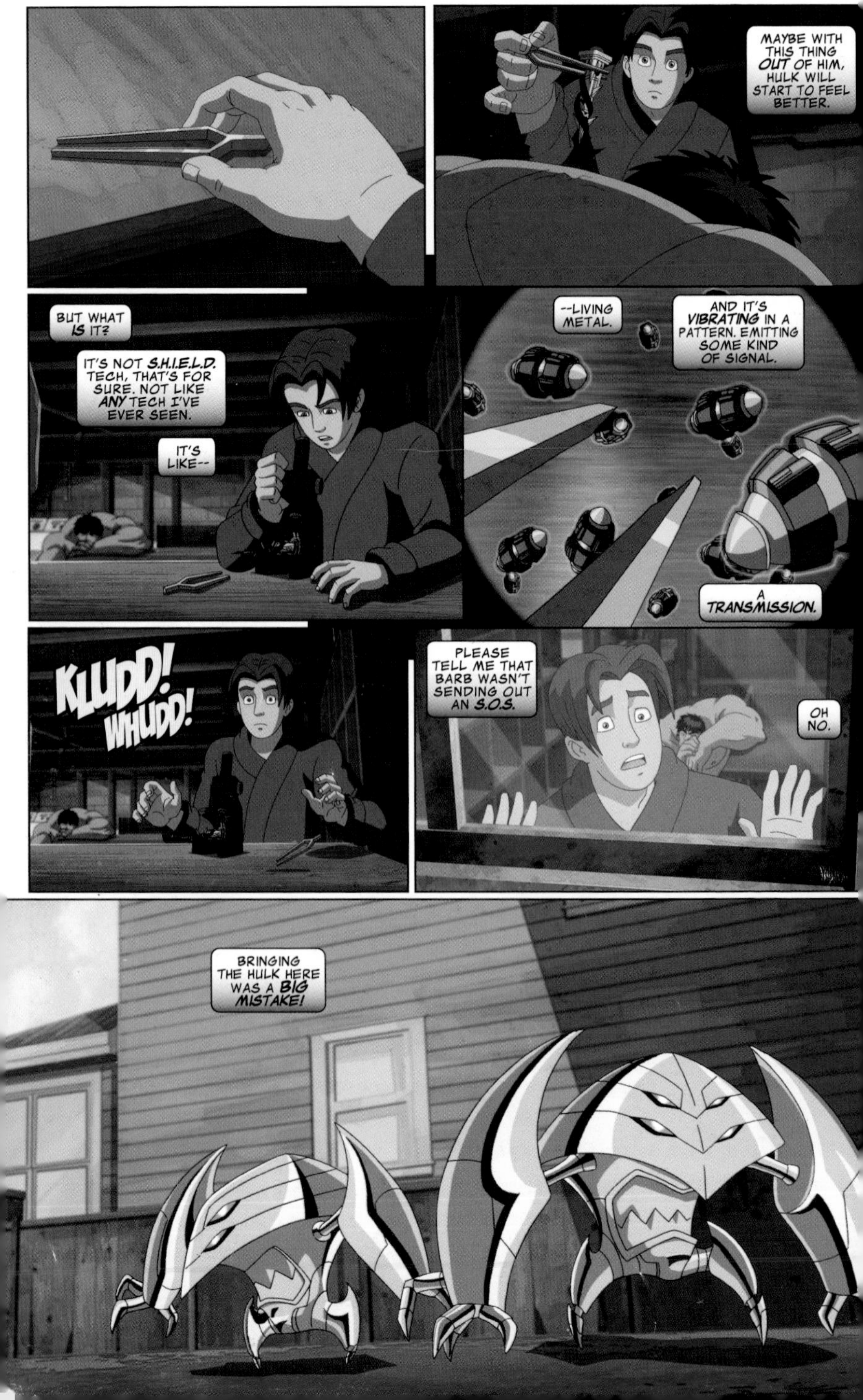

MAYBE WITH THIS THING OUT OF HIM, HULK WILL START TO FEEL BETTER.
BUT WHAT IS IT?
IT'S NOT S.H.I.E.L.D. TECH, THAT'S FOR SURE. NOT LIKE ANY TECH I'VE EVER SEEN.
IT'S LIKE--
--LIVING METAL.
AND IT'S VIBRATING IN A PATTERN. EMITTING SOME KIND OF SIGNAL.
A TRANSMISSION.
KLUDD! WHUDD!
PLEASE TELL ME THAT BARB WASN'T SENDING OUT AN S.O.S.
OH NO.
BRINGING THE HULK HERE WAS A BIG MISTAKE!

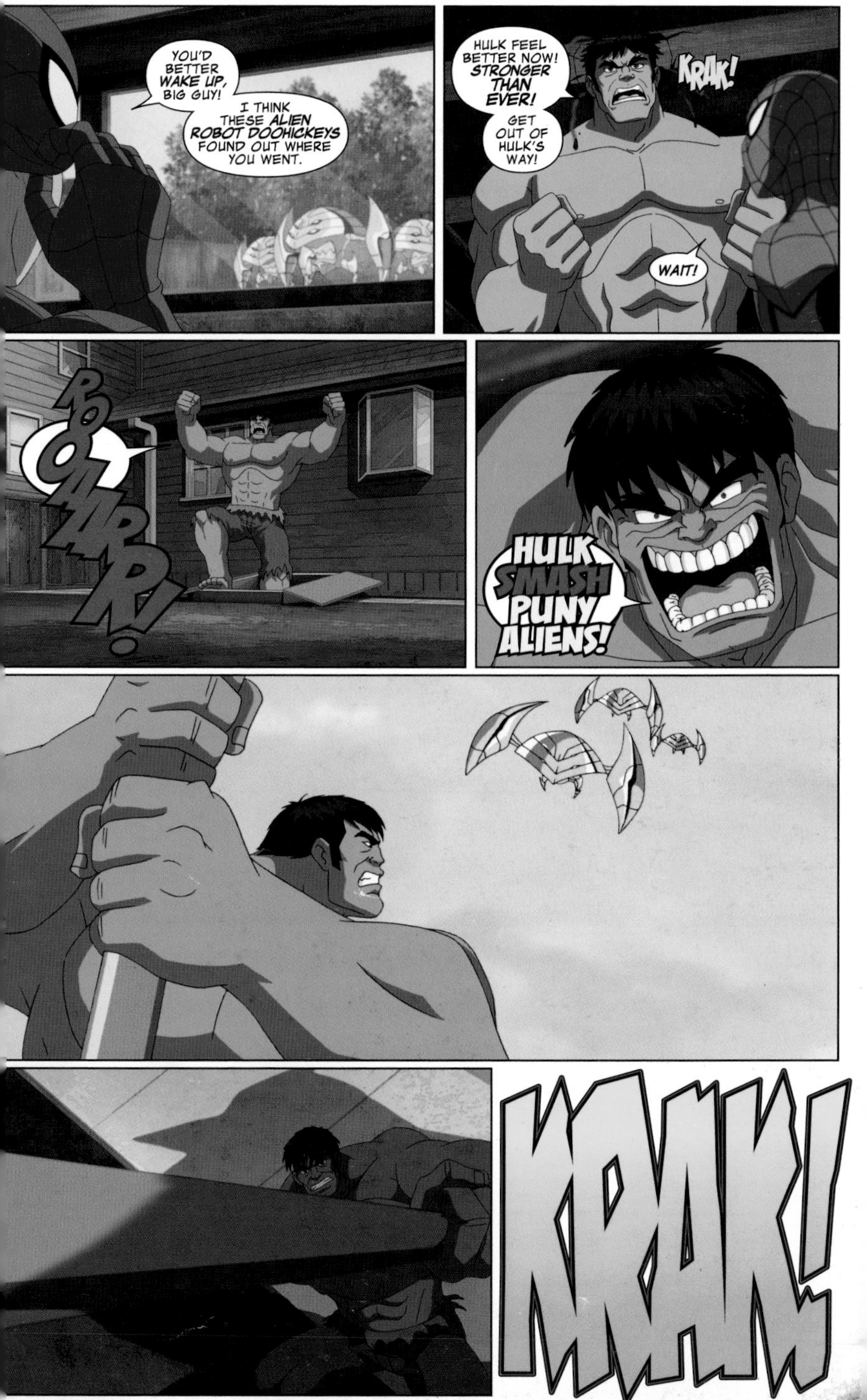
YOU'D BETTER WAKE UP, BIG GUY!
I THINK THESE ALIEN ROBOT DOOHICKEYS FOUND OUT WHERE YOU WENT.
HULK FEEL BETTER NOW! STRONGER THAN EVER!
GET OUT OF HULK'S WAY!
KRAK!
WAIT!
ROOAARR!
HULK SMASH PUNY ALIENS!
KRAK!

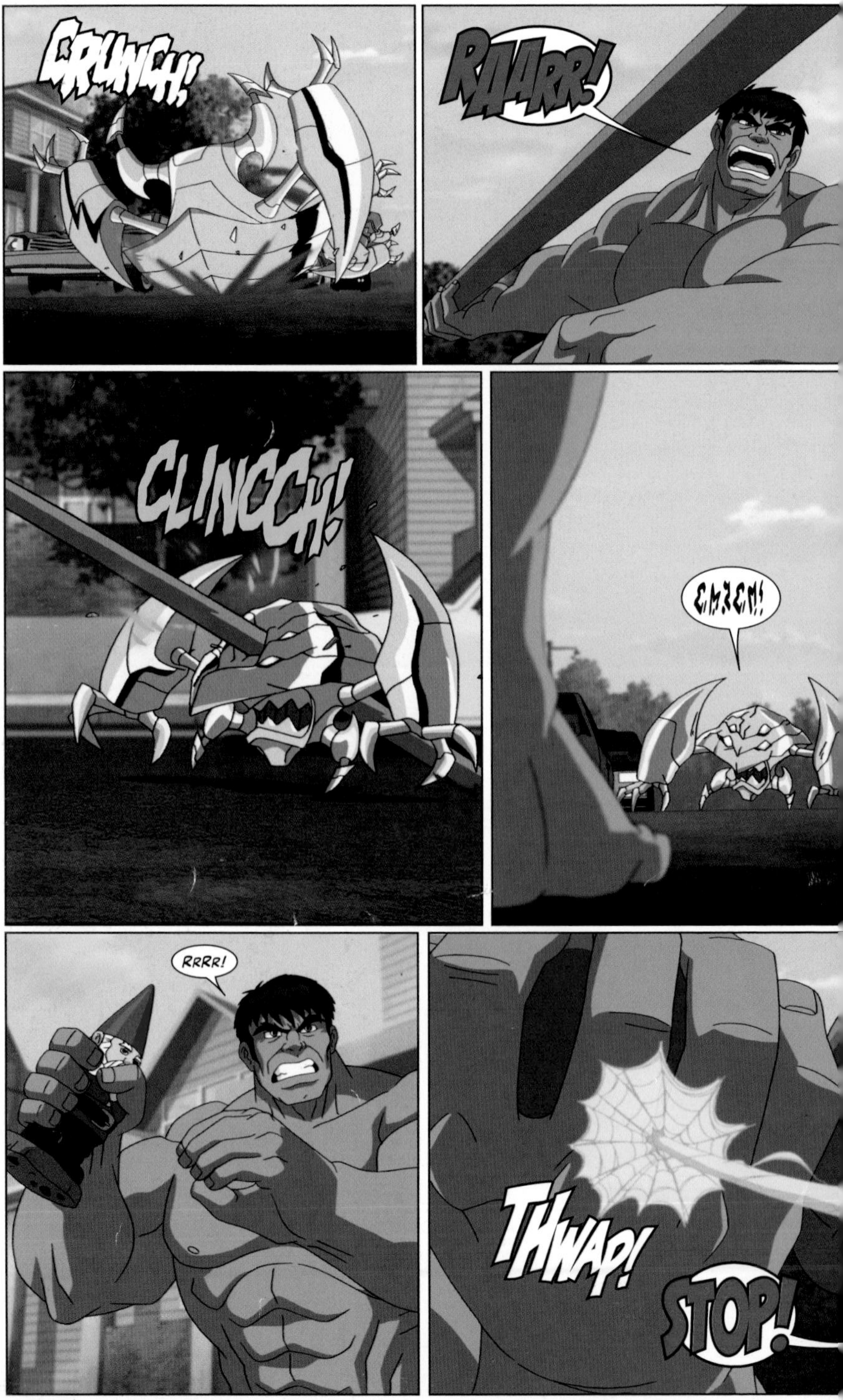
CRUNCH!
RAARR!
CLINCCH!
RRRR!
THWAP!
STOP!

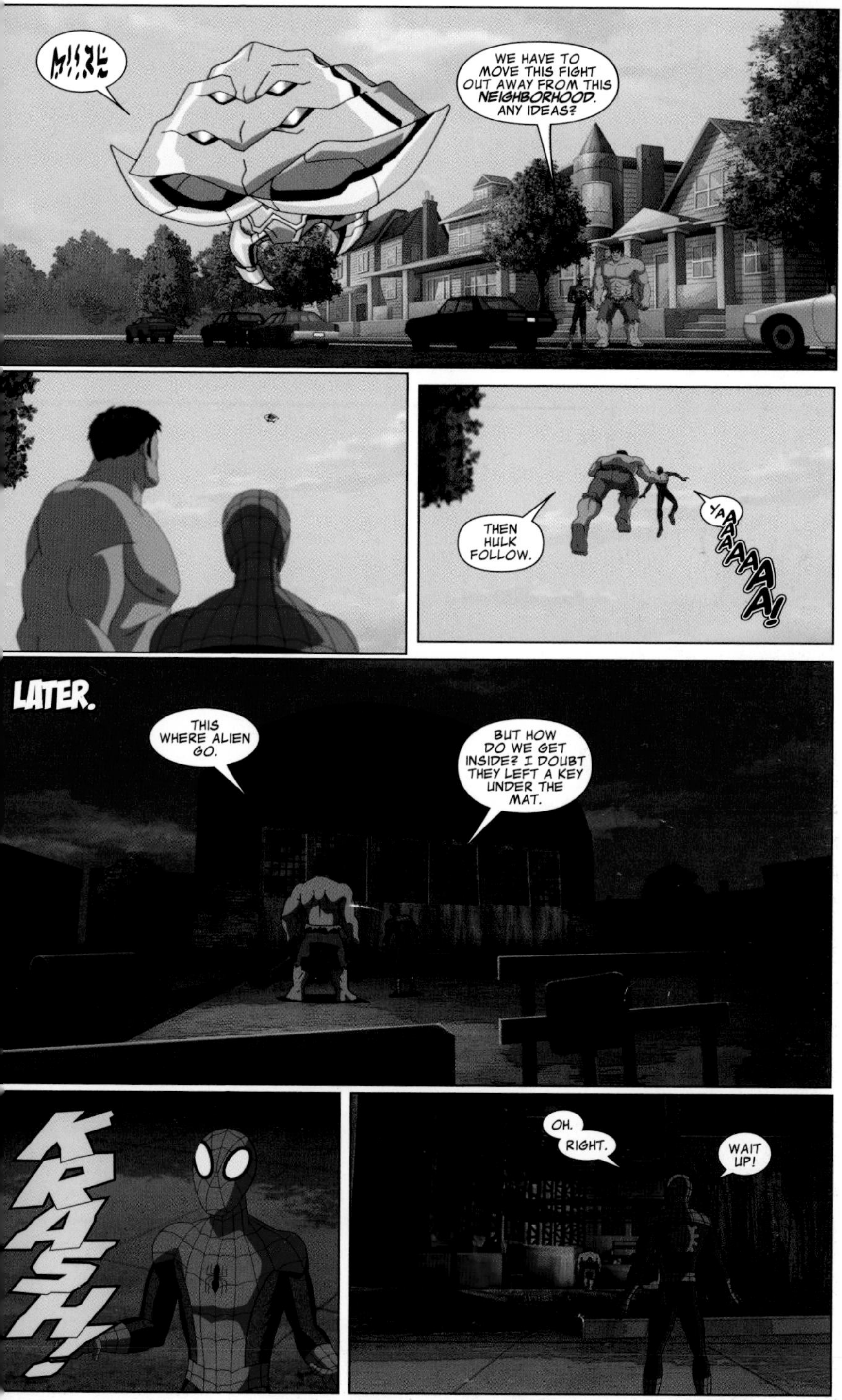

WE HAVE TO MOVE THIS FIGHT OUT AWAY FROM THIS NEIGHBORHOOD. ANY IDEAS?
THEN HULK FOLLOW.
YAAAAAAAA!
LATER.
THIS WHERE ALIEN GO.
BUT HOW DO WE GET INSIDE? I DOUBT THEY LEFT A KEY UNDER THE MAT.
KRASH!
OH.
RIGHT.
WAIT UP!

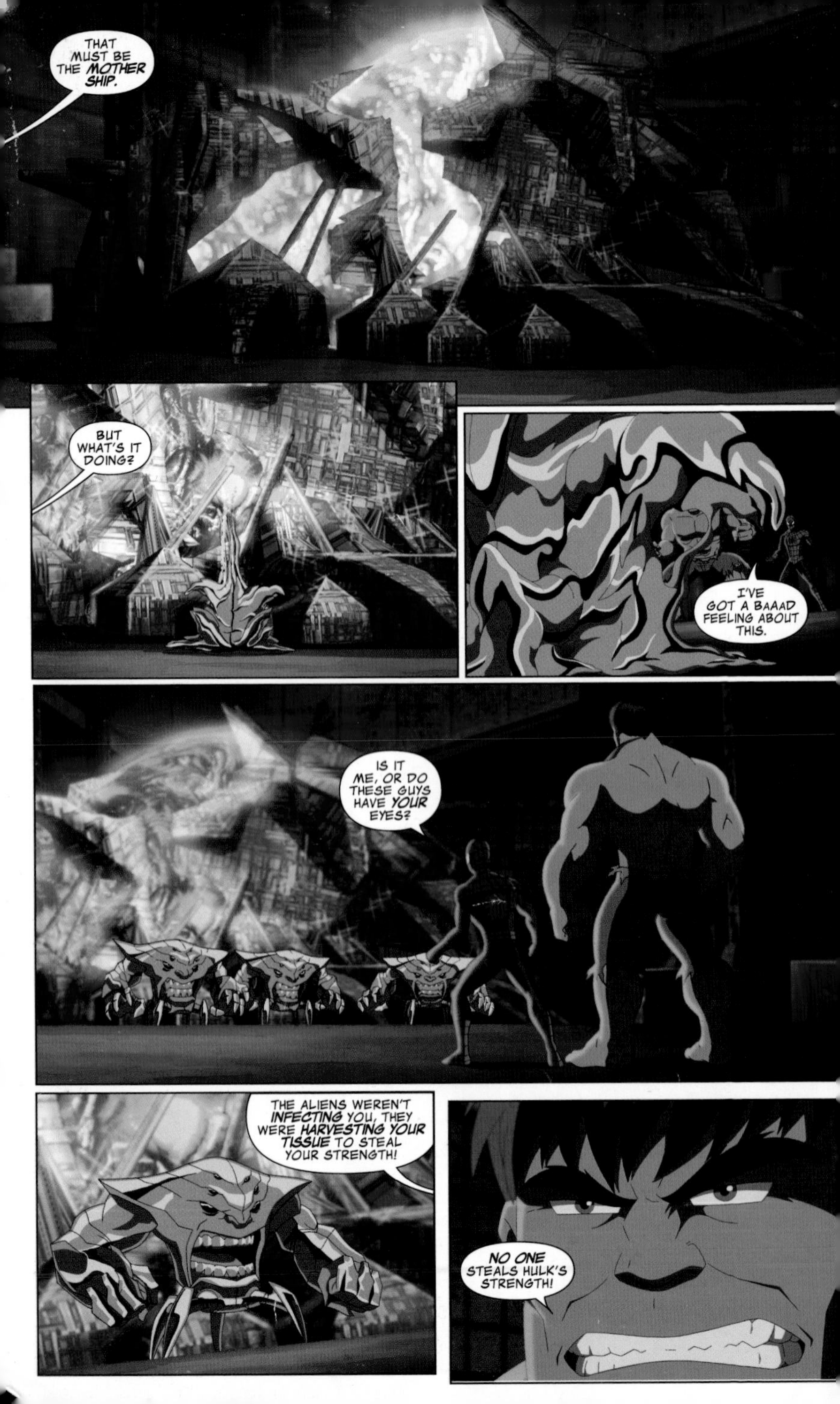
THAT MUST BE THE MOTHER SHIP.
BUT WHAT'S IT DOING?
I'VE GOT A BAAAD FEELING ABOUT THIS.
IS IT ME, OR DO THESE GUYS HAVE YOUR EYES?
THE ALIENS WEREN'T INFECTING YOU, THEY WERE HARVESTING YOUR TISSUE TO STEAL YOUR STRENGTH!
NO ONE STEALS HULK'S STRENGTH!

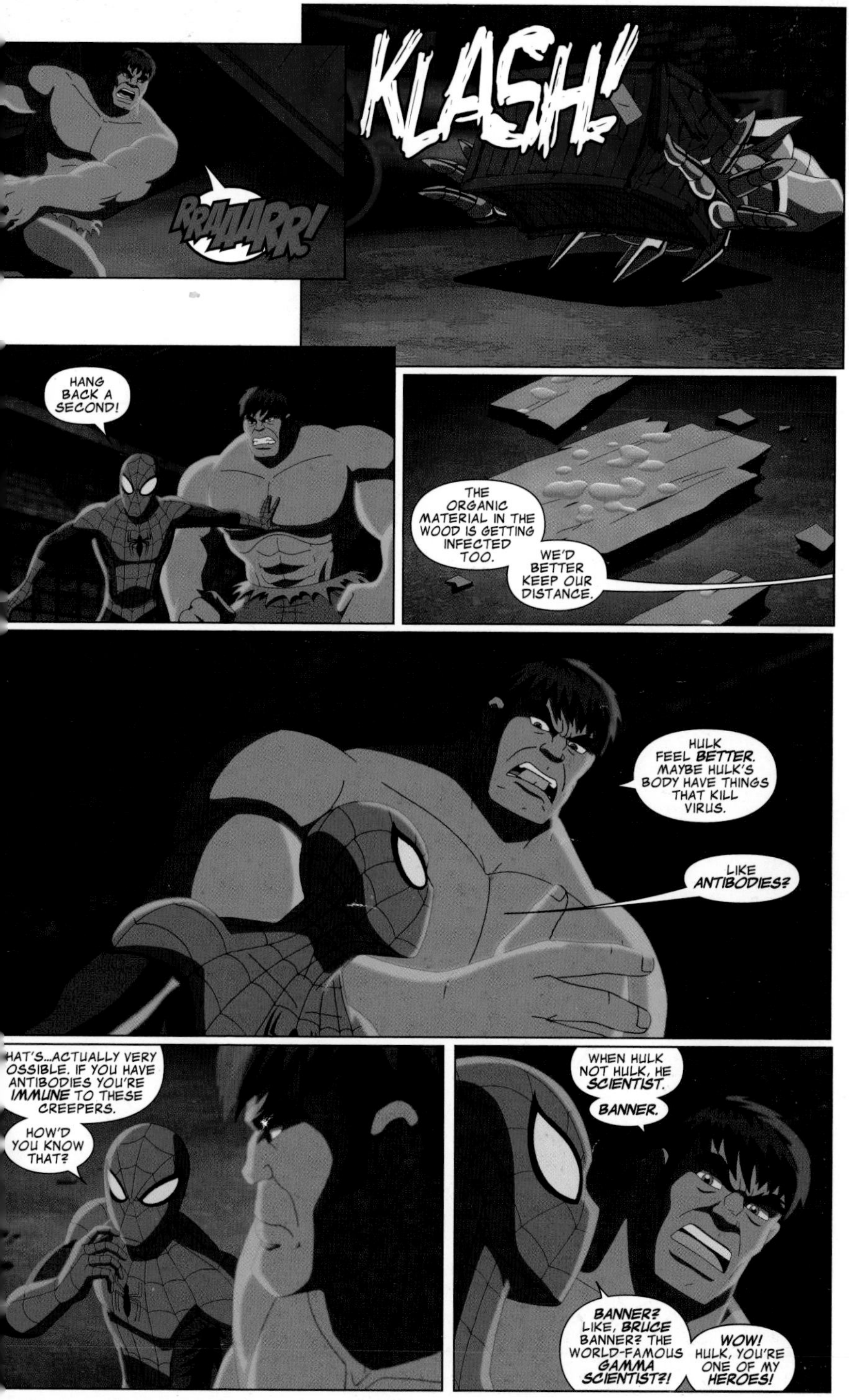
RRAAARR!
KLASH!
HANG BACK A SECOND!
THE ORGANIC MATERIAL IN THE WOOD IS GETTING INFECTED TOO.
WE'D BETTER KEEP OUR DISTANCE.
HULK FEEL BETTER. MAYBE HULK'S BODY HAVE THINGS THAT KILL VIRUS.
LIKE ANTIBODIES?
HAT'S...ACTUALLY VERY OSSIBLE. IF YOU HAVE ANTIBODIES YOU'RE IMMUNE TO THESE CREEPERS.
HOW'D YOU KNOW THAT?
WHEN HULK NOT HULK, HE SCIENTIST.
BANNER.
BANNER? LIKE, BRUCE BANNER? THE WORLD-FAMOUS GAMMA SCIENTIST?!
WOW! HULK, YOU'RE ONE OF MY HEROES!

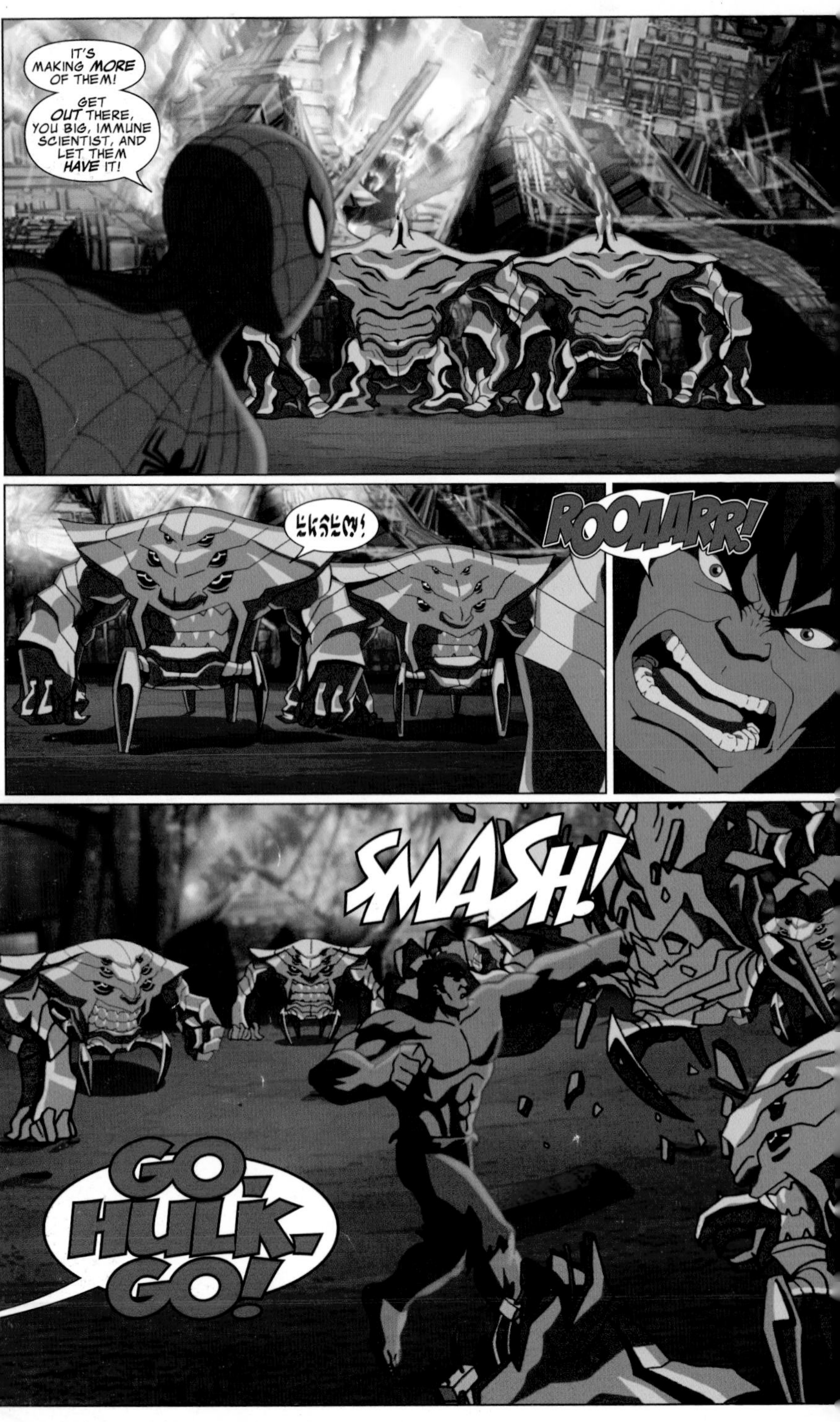
IT'S MAKING MORE OF THEM!
GET OUT THERE, YOU BIG, IMMUNE SCIENTIST, AND LET THEM HAVE IT!
ROOAARR!
SMASH!
GO, HULK, GO!

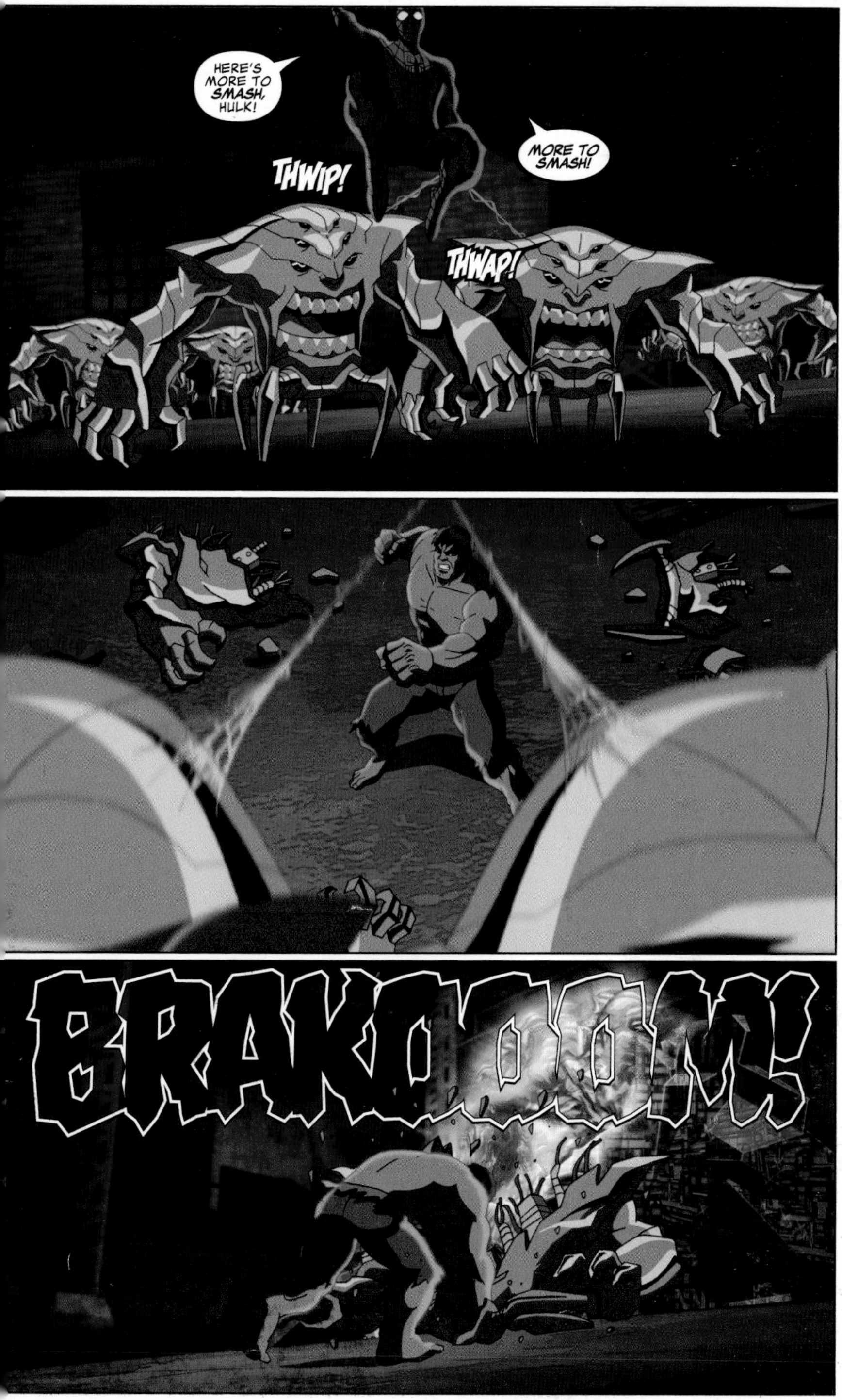
HERE'S MORE TO SMASH, HULK!
MORE TO SMASH!
THWIP!
THWAP!
BRAKOOOM!

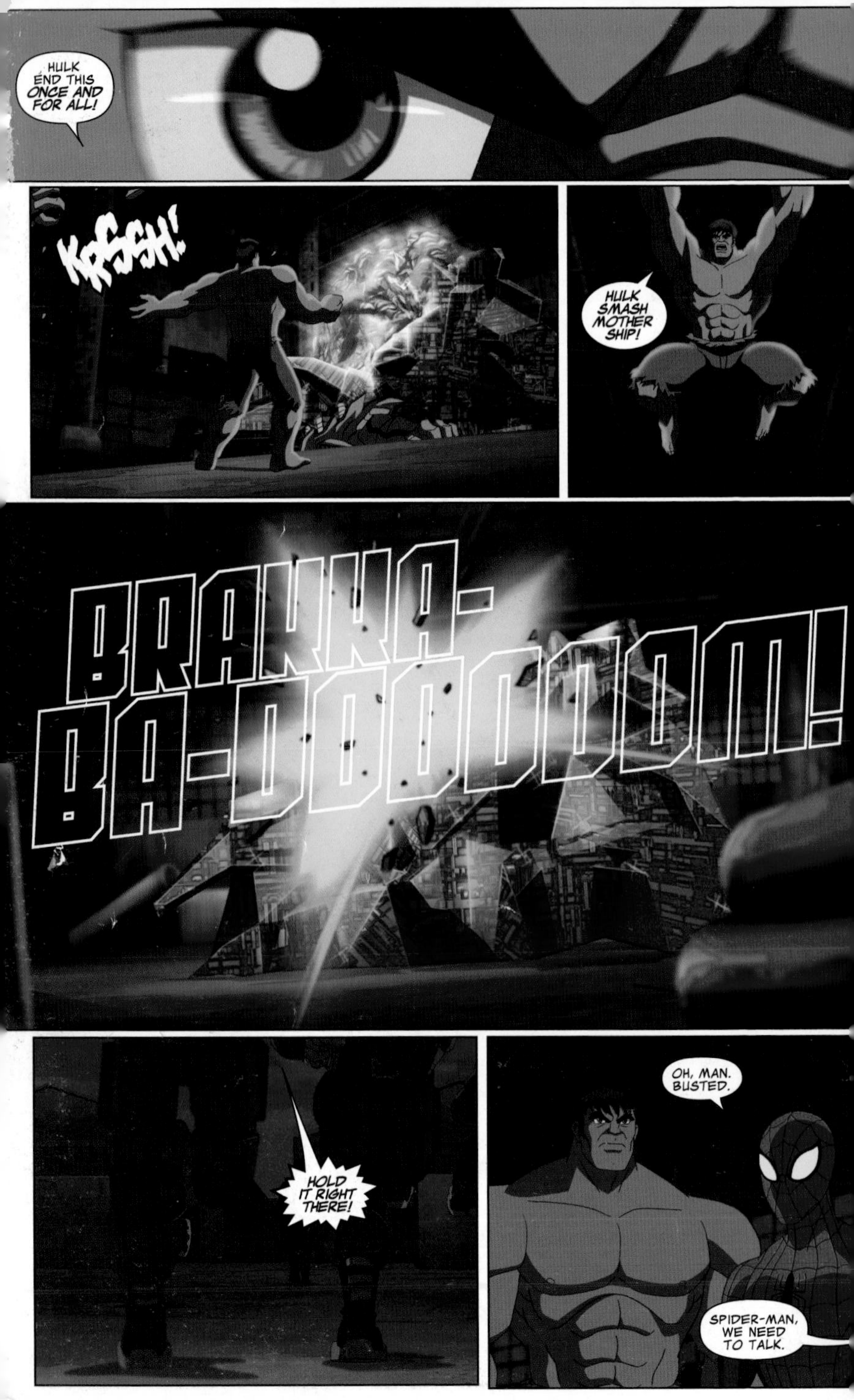
HULK END THIS ONCE AND FOR ALL!
KRSSH!
HULK SMASH MOTHER SHIP!
BRAKKA-BA-DOOOOOM!
HOLD IT RIGHT THERE!
OH, MAN. BUSTED.
SPIDER-MAN, WE NEED TO TALK.

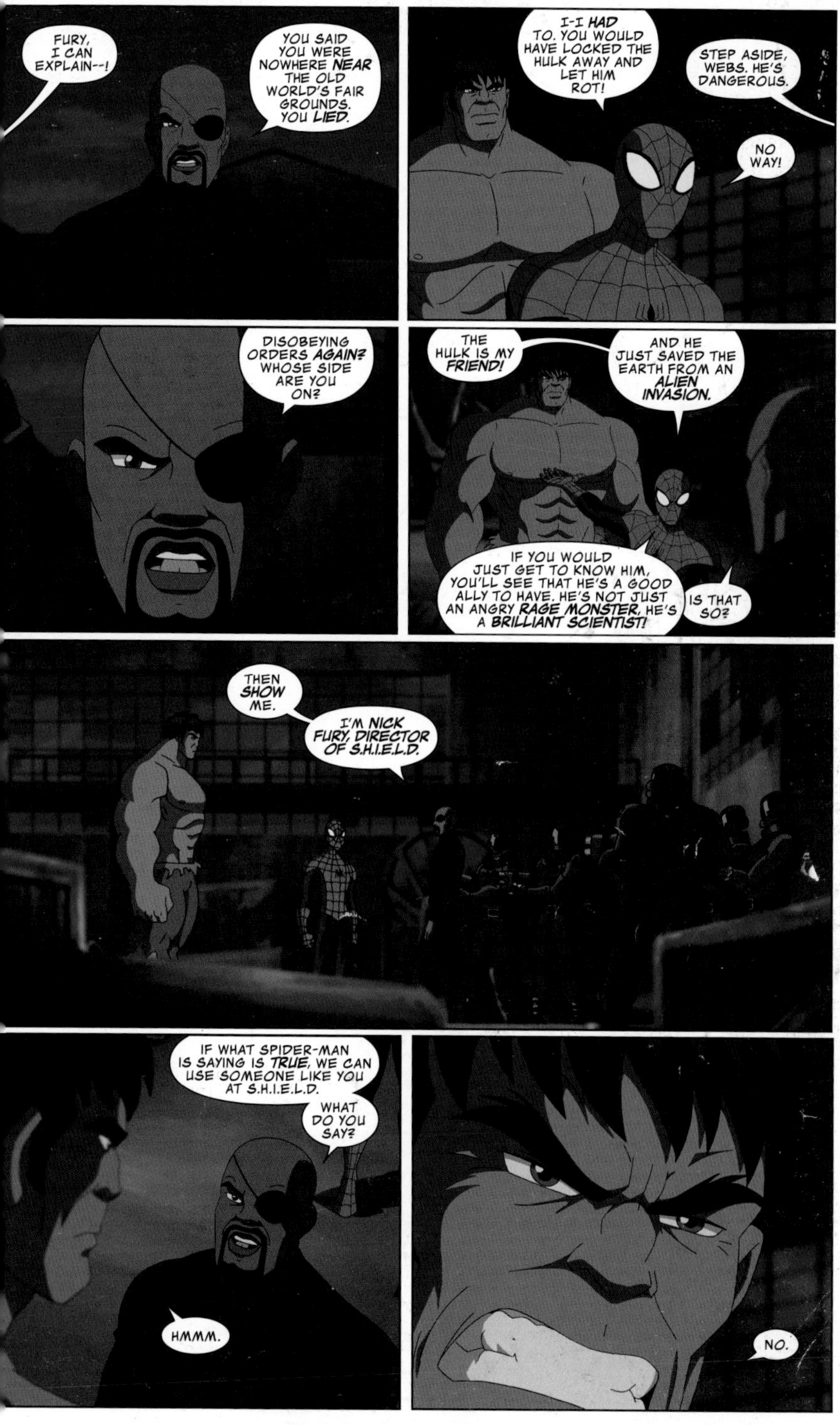
FURY, I CAN EXPLAIN--!
YOU SAID YOU WERE NOWHERE NEAR THE OLD WORLD'S FAIR GROUNDS. YOU LIED.
I-I HAD TO. YOU WOULD HAVE LOCKED THE HULK AWAY AND LET HIM ROT!
STEP ASIDE, WEBS. HE'S DANGEROUS.
NO WAY!
DISOBEYING ORDERS AGAIN? WHOSE SIDE ARE YOU ON?
THE HULK IS MY FRIEND!
AND HE JUST SAVED THE EARTH FROM AN ALIEN INVASION.
IF YOU WOULD JUST GET TO KNOW HIM, YOU'LL SEE THAT HE'S A GOOD ALLY TO HAVE. HE'S NOT JUST AN ANGRY RAGE MONSTER, HE'S A BRILLIANT SCIENTIST!
IS THAT SO?
THEN SHOW ME.
I'M NICK FURY, DIRECTOR OF S.H.I.E.L.D.
IF WHAT SPIDER-MAN IS SAYING IS TRUE, WE CAN USE SOMEONE LIKE YOU AT S.H.I.E.L.D.
WHAT DO YOU SAY?
HMMM.
NO.

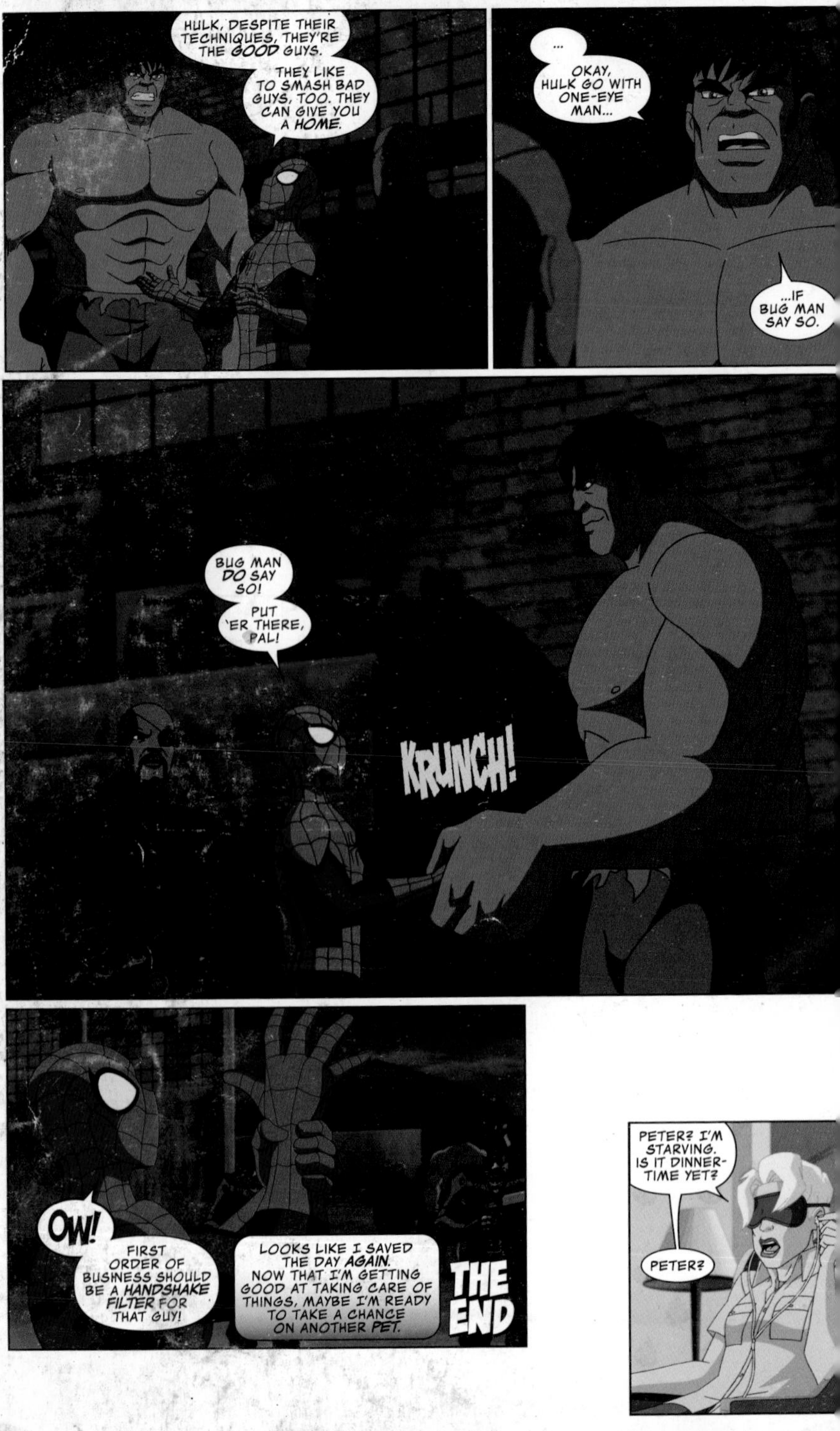
HULK, DESPITE THEIR TECHNIQUES, THEY'RE THE *GOOD* GUYS.
THEY LIKE TO SMASH BAD GUYS, TOO. THEY CAN GIVE YOU A *HOME*.
...
OKAY, HULK GO WITH ONE-EYE MAN...
...IF BUG MAN SAY SO.
BUG MAN *DO* SAY SO!
PUT 'ER THERE, PAL!
KRUNCH!
OW!
FIRST ORDER OF BUSINESS SHOULD BE A *HANDSHAKE FILTER* FOR THAT GUY!
LOOKS LIKE I SAVED THE DAY *AGAIN*. NOW THAT I'M GETTING GOOD AT TAKING CARE OF THINGS, MAYBE I'M READY TO TAKE A CHANCE ON ANOTHER *PET*.
THE END
PETER? I'M STARVING. IS IT DINNER-TIME YET?
PETER?